W9-BLD-097

SHAMBHALA LIBRARY

The Erotic Spirit

AN ANTHOLOGY OF POEMS
OF SENSUALITY, LOVE,
AND LONGING

Edited by
Sam Hamill

SHAMBHALA
Boston & London
2003

FRONTISPIECE: Persian miniature depicting lovers. Free Library of Philadelphia, Pennsylvania. © Scala / Art Resource, New York.

SHAMBHALA PUBLICATIONS, INC.
Horticultural Hall
300 Massachusetts Avenue
Boston, Massachusetts 02115
www.shambhala.com

© 1996 by Sam Hamill

Pages 205–208 constitute an extension of this copyright page.

All rights reserved. No part of this book may be
reproduced in any form or by any means, electronic or
mechanical, including photocopying, recording, or by
any information storage and retrieval system, without
permission in writing from the publisher.

9 8 7 6 5 4 3 2 1

First Shambhala Library Edition
PRINTED IN GERMANY
⊖ This edition is printed on acid-free paper that meets the
American National Standards Institute z39.48 Standard.
Distributed in the United States by Random House, Inc.,
and in Canada by Random House of Canada Ltd

Library of Congress Cataloging-in-Publication Data
The erotic spirit: an anthology of poems of sensuality, love,
and longing/edited by Sam Hamill.
p.   cm.
ISBN 0-87773-957-9 (alk. paper)
ISBN 1-57062-234-5 (pbk.)
ISBN 1-59030-005-x (Shambhala Library edition)
1. Erotic poetry.   I. Hamill, Sam.
PN6110.E65E76   1995   95-15438
808.81'93538—dc20   CIP

To my wife, Gray Foster,
and to my daughter, Eron Hamill

CONTENTS

RUFINUS (ca. 2nd century BCE?)

MARCUS ARGENTARIUS (ca. 60 BCE)

CATULLUS (ca. 84–54 BCE)

PHILODEMOS (fl. 75–35 BCE)

OVID (43 BCE–17 CE)

PETRONIUS ARBITER (d. 66 CE)

TZU YEH (4th century)

AGATHIAS SCHOLASTICUS (ca. 531–580)

PREFACE

THIRTY-FIVE CENTURIES ago, an Egyptian poet sat down under a sycamore tree and gazed out at a river where hungry crocodiles were sunning themselves on sandbars. And as he thought about his feelings for his beloved, who lived on the other shore, he composed a poem:

> The little sycamore she planted
> prepares to speak—the sound of rustling leaves
> sweeter than honey.
>
> On its lovely limbs
> is new fruit and ripe fruit red as blood jasper,
> and leaves of green jasper.
>
> Her love awaits me on the distant shore.
> The river flows between us,
> crocodiles on the sandbars.
>
> Yet I plunge into the river,
> my heart slicing currents, steady
> as if I were walking.
>
> O my love, it is love
> that gives me strength and courage,
> love that fords the river.

A thousand years after the writing of this poem, a Greek thinker would observe: "The soul, to know itself, must gaze into a soul." And that is exactly the place to begin a reading of poems articulating the erotic spirit, poetry rooted in the experience of interpenetrating fleshly and spiritual delight.

The word *erotic* comes from Eros, ancient Greek god of love, a mischievous trickster given to indulging in cruel pranks, but who remains forever seductive, young, and beautiful. Eros was a major deity in a number of mystery cults and represented the embodiment of desire. He was the son of the goddess of love, beauty, and fertility, Aphrodite, whom Hesiod said rose up from the seafoam (*aphros*); Homer called her "the Kyprian"; Plato said she symbolizes intellectual as well as sexual love; modern scholars trace her origins back to the Asian goddess Astarte.

Our Egyptian poet discovers within himself a love so profound it moves him to risk life and limb, a love larger than life. He's never heard of the Greek god or goddess of love, and has his own gods and goddesses and little godlets of adoration to attend. He longs to let his body and her body become one, unified by love as soul searches soul until self is transcended and they come to know, in a moment of passion and tender compassion, the very face of God. But how to know the self-indulgent desires of the flesh from the truest spiritual connections that transcend selfish impulses? Poets have wrestled with this equation since the dawn of language. One way to attempt resolution is to explore poetry of the erotic spirit as a handbook, a guidebook for care of the lover's soul.

Desire confounds us, Buddhist, Christian, Muslim, Jew, atheist, pantheist, agnostic . . . desire confounds us. Our vocabulary of the erotic spirit is often impoverished. Denis de Rougemont, in *Love in the Western World,* divides love into two types: "Christian love," or agape, a love between equals concluding in a marriage for the purpose of procreation; and eros, a love between "unequal" persons, rooted in passion, rejecting marriage, and growing ever more passionate through separation of the lovers. De Rougemont claims eros entered Western civilization only through the Catharist heresy of the twelfth century. By my reckoning, he missed the mark by about eighteen centuries. Still, he is right when he claims a devotional foundation for the poetry, a poetics in which the Lady of the poem is representative of Sancta Maria Sophia, figure of eternal wisdom and "bride of God." In this context, the longing for the perfection of love, for its spiritual realization as well as for its embodiment, is a longing for a physical manifestation of God's love and follows an attitude of adoration established in the "Song of Songs." It took an Inquisition to expel belief in such "heresies."

The most universally influential anthology of poems of the erotic spirit, "The Song of Songs," a collection with roots in Hebrew, Aramaic, Greek, and

Egyptian, is an epithalamion, a marriage ceremony in verse, a celebration of the sanctity of the erotic spirit of love between partners. The lovers are "equal" *and* erotically inspired. More than just a collection of poems, "The Song of Songs" has come to be a single suite that is larger than the sum of its parts, sequential in gathering power as phrases or images recur. It establishes familial connections. The bride is also a "sister," as are the women who bear witness; and the groom is a "brother," as are all men present. The bride says:

> I return from the wilderness
> on the arm of my belovéd whom I awakened
> under the apple tree
> where his mother bore him.

The groom then is a son of Eve who ate the apple of knowledge and was suddenly shamed by her nakedness and expelled from the perfect garden. The bride has found her groom not in Eden, but in the "wilderness" that is also a wilderness of the imagination. She returns with him to her family and its own garden, the praises of which both shall sing. The garden in such a context becomes a replica or an interpretation of Eden. The bride marries the son of the first mother, the mother of all mothers. The bride is variously described as a "wall" and a "door" and offers the "vineyard of [herself]." She becomes the embodiment of the garden as wife (*wyf* originating in "veiled woman") and is joined to husband (a *husbandman* is "one who patrols boundaries"). Her veil represents the mystery of the garden before love's labors inform its many possibilities. She is a door opening a future, a wall defining boundaries.

Beyond the beauty of rich procreative metaphor in the poem lies the intricate web of devotional love— between lovers, family, community, and God. The garden of the poem is not Eden, but a vineyard, a garden that must be a focus of labor to produce and sustain the wealth and happiness of the household. The garden interprets Eden, the work preparing the couple for the heavenly garden of the next life.

But if there is a heaven, there is also a hell, and there is also a terrible side of the erotic spirit. Few express it as well as Gaius Valerius Catullus (84–54 CE) who is fond of echoing the ecstatic lines of Sappho while turning them to his own ends, often in an expression of frustration or plainspoken anger.

> Your sins have brought my mind so low,
> my Lesbia, you damn even my devotion.
> I can neither praise your rare benevolence,
> nor love you less for your excesses.

Catullus understands something about the nature of devotion, a lot about passion, but he cannot master the sacred. He becomes a paradigm for all the tortured lovers who will follow him down the centuries, passionately proclaiming his love while simultaneously complaining that his beloved will not change her behavior to his satisfaction. In his own way, Catullus accepts her as she is, happily complaining and proclaiming his devotion all the way, a brilliant albeit decadent poet in a decadent time.

All cultures produce "erotic art" of many kinds, expressing the erotic spirit in poetry, visual arts, music, and dance. From the tantric Buddhist texts of India to Taoist love manuals to the *Gnostic Gospels,* the erotic spirit has been expressed in inventiveness, in constant discovery in the play of ceremonial (religious) devotion. In the love of the dark lord Krishna for the milkmaid Radha or of the ecstatic Mirabai for Krishna, in the love of Zen master Ikkyu for his Lady Mori or the poems of Robert Herrick, we find again and again the expression of love in which any distinction between the religious or spiritual and the carnal are utterly obliterated. Kenneth Rexroth has written, "Erotic love is one of the highest forms of contemplation."

The great Chinese poets of the T'ang dynasty would draw, on the one hand, from the Buddhist tradition and, on the other, from the Taoist tradition that goes at least as far back as the Yellow Emperor's writing of the first sex manual (2700 BCE). "To understand the head, investigate as well the tail." The fundamental tenet of Taoism is the balancing of *yin* and *yang,* feminine and masculine principles, to achieve a harmonious whole bound together by the unnameable third power. A famous Taoist sex manual by Tung Hsuan Tzu, *Art of the*

Bedchamber, advises the male, among other things, to hold back climax until the woman has "burst the cloud," and offers instruction on how to do so. The Taoist tradition is rich with recipes for aphrodisiacs, sacred erotic ritual, sex manuals to educate and to entertain. By the time of the Chou dynasty (eleventh century BCE) the commissioning of poems and stories was common court practice, and themes of love lost and love won were among the most popular.

In the Buddhist tradition, poetry addressing the erotic spirit most often deals in one way or another with a sense of longing. Buddhism teaches the importance of not being overcome with desire, of not clinging. In the Zen tradition that dominates the classical poetry of China and Japan, Buddhist practice is centered in silent solitary self-illumination, whereby one transcends possessiveness, ego-driven desire, and other destructive attitudes that contribute to a very large degree to domestic disharmony. Compassion and affection are stressed. But Zen mind is not an exclusively transcendental mind. Zen mind gets up in the morning to take a leak. Zen mind plants rice and beans, washes clothes, changes diapers, makes dinner, all within the framework of the sacred erotic spirit of love, loving the work and play within a familial devotion that does not exclude sexuality. Poets in this tradition often associate erotic longing with a desire for enlightenment. Izumi Shikibu (970–1030) writes:

> When I think of you,
> fireflies in the marsh rise
> like the soul's jewels,
> lost to eternal longing,
> abandoning my body

She associates being with her lover with a sense of "abandoning" her body. Her erotic love is connected to a transcendent state, or at least to an *aspect* of that state. It is as natural and as astonishing and mysterious as fireflies—bodies of light—in the mist and damp darkness of the marsh. The soul's jewels—moments of brilliant light in the life of the soul—are recovered and are equally natural, however rare. The hardness of jewels may be contrasted with the softness of the marsh, the male and the female. The figures of light correspond to spiritual enlightenment. She has glimpsed Nirvana.

The sacred erotic spirit is celebrated in every culture. It should not be surprising to note the number of poets famous for their erotic vision who are associated with rigorous spiritual practice: Sappho, the poets of the Song of Songs, Dante, Petrarch, Rumi, Kabir, Ikkyu, Vidyapati, Mirabai, Herrick, Sor Juana Inés de la Cruz, and Blake all celebrate the erotic spirit as part of the sacred tradition. For the poet, the very act of making the poem is an act of divination, a sacred practice. Octavio Paz has written, "The agent that provokes both the erotic act and the poetic act is imagination. Imagination turns sex into ceremony and rite, language into rhythm and metaphor. The poetic image is an embrace of opposite realities, and rhyme a copulation of sounds; poetry eroticizes language and the world because its operation is erotic to begin with."

In our own time, we are fortunate to have an abundance of truly remarkable poets, although we as Americans seem to be the last on earth to acknowledge this gift. All over the world, the literary minded are going to school on contemporary American poets, and one of the reasons is that our poets have opened the doors to the world's many poetic traditions, finding in translation into American English poetry that articulates our deepest needs and desires, that celebrates our fundamental joys, that, like the erotic spirit, achieves its maximum realization only as it is given freely away.

In selecting original poems and poems for translation for this book, I have held in mind the Greek roots of our word "anthology"—*anthos,* meaning flower (which may be related to the Sanskrit *andha,* meaning herb), and *logos,* meaning gathering. The anthology is a garland, a flower-gathering, and I have woven these various strands chronologically in hopes of revealing general developments and attitudes over the centuries. Such a garland is personal rather than comprehensive, and yet in many ways representative, spanning many cultures and epochs.

ACKNOWLEDGEMENTS

SPECIAL THANKS are due to Kenneth Rexroth, who, thirty years ago, recommended erotic poetry to me as "a lifetime's study"; to the late William Arrowsmith, who encouraged and often corrected my translations from ancient Greek; to J. P. Seaton, fellow poet and Chinese scholar, for years of help and friendship; to Olga Broumas, who best embodies and encourages the Sapphic spirit in our time; and to my editor, Peter Turner, for keeping faith while helping me find my way.

The Erotic Spirit

Anonymous Egyptian

(ca. 15th–10th centuries BCE)

THE little sycamore she planted
prepares to speak—the sound of rustling leaves
sweeter than honey.

On its lovely green limbs
is new fruit and ripe fruit red as blood jasper,
and leaves of green jasper.

Her love awaits me on the distant shore.
The river flows between us,
crocodiles on the sandbars.

Yet I plunge into the river,
my heart slicing currents, steady
as if I were walking.

O my love, it is love
that gives me strength and courage,
love that fords the river.

My lover is a lotus blossom
with pomegranate breasts;
her face is a polished wooden snare.

And I am the poor wild bird
seduced
into the teeth of her trap.

HE is the love-wolf
gobbling in my cave,
within . . . the pebbles beneath
. . . the moringa tree

. . . eating of the bread
offered to the gods

(translated by Barbara Hughes Fowler)

Sappho
(6th century BCE)

He is almost a god, a man beside you,
enthralled by your talk, by your laughter.
Watching makes my heart beat fast
because, seeing little, I imagine much.
You put a fire in my cheeks.
Speech won't come. My ears ring.
Blind to all others, I sweat and I stammer.
I am a trembling thing, like grass,
an inch from dying.

So poor I've nothing to lose, I must gamble . . .

I LOVE
love's delicacy.

Love offers me
this brilliant sun,

the virtue
of its beauty.

Eros seizes and shakes my very soul
like the wind on the mountain
shaking ancient oaks.

Anakreon

(ca. 570 BCE)

WEAVING a garland long ago,
somehow I found Eros
there among the roses.

I clutched him by his wings
and thrust him into wine
and drank him quickly.

And ever since, deep inside,
I feel the wings of Eros
gently tickling.

Asklepiados

(ca. 320 BCE)

THINK how unspeakably sweet
the taste of snow at midsummer,
how sweet a kind spring breeze
after the gales of winter.

But as we all discover,
nothing's quite as sweet
as one large cloak
wrapped around two lovers.

DIDYME waved an olive branch at me,
and now my heart melts like wax
embraced by flame.

Oh, I know, I know. She is dark.
And so's the coal before the spark
that makes it burn like roses.

from

The Song of Songs

(ca. 3rd century BCE)

SHE

Give me all the kisses of your mouth.
Your love is better than wine.

Your body oils are fragrant,
your name pours from my tongue.
That is why I adore you.

Call me and I will follow,
and enter the chambers of a king.

Together we celebrate love,
a love more fragrant than wine.
Oh, how I adore you!

HE

O daughter of Jerusalem,
like the tents of Kedar and the curtains of a king,
I am the Dark One.
Turn away your eyes.

I am the strong one browned by desert suns.
My mother's sons despised me

and sent me to work their vineyards
while my own remained untamed.

You whom my soul adores, I'll tell you where
I take my meal, where I nap at noon—
Leave your veil of modesty behind
and stand revealed.

Most beautiful woman!
Follow the trails of my flock;
feed the kids that bleat
behind the shepherds' tents.

Like the beautiful horse that draws
the Pharaoh's chariot, my love,
your cheeks are jeweled,
your throat ringed with gold.

I shall bring you
three golden rings with silver studs.

SHE

1

With the king at his table,
my winecup overflows with fragrance.

You are, my love, a bag of myrrh between my
   breasts,
a cluster of henna in the vineyards of Engedi.

You are fair, my love, you are so fair,
and your eyes are the eyes of the dove.

You are so fair, my love, and so pleasing,
and our couch is soft and leafy.

May the beams of our home be carved from cedar,
our rafters from sturdy cypress.

2

I am a rose of Sharon,
a lily of the valley,
a lily among thorns,
as is my love among others.

My beloved is a flowering apple
blooming in the forest.
I delight in his shadow,
his sweet fruits nourish me.

He brought me to the banquet of his house
with his banner above me;
he stayed me with flagons and apples
for I am starved for his love.

His left hand lifts my head
while his right hand embraces.

O daughters of Jerusalem,
do not disturb him,
leave him to dream of gazelles in the field,
do not disturb his dreaming.

The voice of my love is a song
leaping from hill to mountain
like a gazelle,
bounding, leaping over hills.

My beloved has stood beyond our wall
to peek into my window,
and he peered through the lattice
and sang to me softly.

"Rise, my love, my beautiful one.
The winter is past and the rains have gone
and flowers cover the world
and the time for our singing has come.

"You are my dove, high up among the stones
in the recesses of the cliff.
I long to see your face, I long for your sweet voice,
your face so lovely, your song divine.

"Listen for the voice of the turtledove.
The fig bursts with new buds
and the vineyards blossom sweetly.
Rise up, my love, and come away with me."

3

I am my love's; my beloved is mine.
We lie among lilies until daybreak
drives away the shadows.

Turn to me, my love,
like the gazelle of your dreams,
leaping through mountains of spices.

4

My soul sought him out at night in my bed,
sought him, but could not find him.
And I rose to search through the city—
through alleyways and avenues,
I searched for the love of my life.

I searched, I sought, but could not find him.
When the city watchmen passed, I begged,
"Have you seen him who is my soul's delight?"

And then I found him and held him fast
and clutched him to my heart and clung
until he came into my mother's house,
into the boudoir where I was conceived.

O daughters of Zion, by all the gazelles of the field,
I warn you, do not stir love until its time has come.

5

Who is it appears out of the wilderness,
a pillar of smoke perfumed with frankincense
    and myrrh,
with the powders and ointments of a merchant?

Ah, it is his litter
surrounded by sixty valiant men
of Israel, each with his sword,

each expert in the arts of war.
But every sword on every thigh is there
because fear haunts the night.

He has made a palaquin from cedars of Lebanon,
he has plated the pillars with silver
and the frame with gold.

Inside, the daughters of Jerusalem
stitched cushions of lavender blue,
sewn 'round with the threads of love.

Come see him, you daughters of Zion,
see him crowned with his mother's crown
on the morning of his wedding,

on the day his heart is sanctified.

He

Come from Lebanon with me, my love,
and be my bride. Come with me from Lebanon.

Look down from the summits of Amana, Shenir,
    and Hermon,
from the dens of lions and the mountains of leopards.

My heart cries out for you, my bride, my sister who
    has torn
my heart with her eyes like a bead from a necklace.

You are so fair, my sister, my bride; your love
is better than wine, rarer than ointments and spices.

Your lips are milk and honey for my tongue.
From your robes, I breathe the fragrances of
    Lebanon.

You are the garden within the walls, my sister;
a capped spring, my bride, a sealed fountain;

you are a pomegranate forest with exotic fruits,
with henna and spikenard, calamus and cinnamon
    and saffron,

a forest of frankincense, myrrh and aloe;
you are a fountain of gardens,

you are the waters of my very soul,
the sacred living, flowing stream of Lebanon.

SHE

Awaken now, O north wind, arise and blow;
and now, O south wind, blow across my garden;
blow, winds, across my plot of spices;
invite him into my garden
to savor my succulent fruits.

As though you were my brother
who sucked the breast of my mother,
finding you in need, I'd offer kisses,
and who could despise me?

I would bring you into my mother's house
for you to teach me.

I would bring spiced wine
and the juice of pomegranates.

Your left hand should lift my chin
while your right hand caresses.

O daughters of Jerusalem, do not
disturb my love as he sleeps, do not awaken him.

I return from the wilderness
on the arm of my belovéd whom I awakened
under the apple tree
where his mother bore him.

I would be the seal upon your heart,
the seal upon your arm.

Love is stronger than death, jealousy
cruel as a grave flashing fire.

Many waters are not enough to slake the thirst
   of love,
a multitude of floods cannot submerge it.

If a man gives all his household goods for love,
it would not be enough.

HE

We have a little sister, too small for breasts,
but what shall we do for her
on the day when she, our sister, is spoken for?

If she is a wall, we'll build her a turret of silver.
And if she is a door,
we'll frame her with fine cedar.

SHE

I am a wall and my breasts are its towers.
What peace I know, I find only in your eyes.

When Solomon gave his vineyard at Baal-hamon,
he gave it to its keepers;
and now each fruit brings a thousand pieces of silver.

Here is the vineyard of myself.
You who are my Solomon shall have the thousand.

And those who keep the fruit and tend the garden?
Give them two hundred if they will call for your song
and let me hear it.

Be fleet, my love, as the fleet gazelle
deep in the mountains of spices.

Praxilla

(ca. 2nd century BCE?)

PEEKING in through
the open window,
your face was
virginal.

But you were
all woman
below.

Anonymous Greek

(ca. 2nd century BCE?)

WHETHER I see you now
with glistening raven hair

or find you blonde and fair,
I find somehow

in your sweet face
that same grace.

I daresay
the very god of love

will stroke your hair
when it is gray.

Rufinus

(ca. 2nd century BCE?)

HER foot sparkled like silver
splashing bath water
on her golden apple breasts,
grown heavy with their milk.

Her curving hip,
smooth as water, shifted,
making waves, her hand
covering her *mons veneris,*

hiding but a part of it.

How could I have known
Kythereia was in her bath,
her lovely hands letting
her hair laugh about her throat.

May she, my queen, have mercy—
my eyes saw what was not meant for me.
Her unspeakable beauty, her graces
have shamed even the Goddess.

Marcus Argentarius

(ca. 60 BCE)

I CAN'T bear to watch your hips
as you walk away.
          Untie me!
Your thin dress leaves you
nearly naked. You tease
and tease.
       But one suggestion:
dress me, too, in gauze
so you can see
the shadow of my erection.

HER perfect naked breast
upon my breast,
her lips between my lips,

I lay in perfect bliss
with lovely Antigone,
nothing caught between us.

I will not tell the rest.
Only the lamp bore witness.

Catullus

(ca. 84–54 BCE)

H E is like a god,
he is greater than a god
sitting beside you listening
to your laughter. You make me crazy.
Seeing you, my Lesbia, takes my breath away.
My tongue freezes, my body
is filled with flames,
bells ring, and night invades my eyes.
Leisure, Catullus, is your curse.
You exult in it, the very thing
that brought down noble houses and great cities.

My woman says she'd rather have me
than anyone. Even if Jupiter proposed,
she says. But what an eager woman says to lovers
should be written out in winds and waters.

Sᴡᴇᴇᴛ sparrow, my lover's pet
she fondles between her thighs
attacking with long fingers
whenever she hungers for its sharp bite.
I do not know why she should get
such pleasure by hurting her little pet,
the solace which delights her heart.
I wish as well the bite of its beak
could give my troubled soul relief.

Your sins have brought my mind so low,
my Lesbia, you've damned even my devotion.
I can neither praise your rare benevolence,
nor love you less for your excesses.

My LOVELY, sweet Ipsithilla,
my delicious, my passion,
call for me this afternoon.
Please send for me so I may come
without question.
And don't sneak off as I enter.
Stay, and wait, and dream up
nine different kinds of copulation
to keep us entertained.
Send for me here, after lunch,
where I'm supine on my bed
with my cock peeking out from my tunic.

Philodemos

(fl. 75–35 BCE)

XANTHIPPE, singing at her lyre,
with whispering eyes
sets my soul on fire.

But when? Where? How?
Everything's uncertain.
Except that my soul is burning.

Ovid

(43 BCE–17 CE)

Elegy to His Mistress

IN summer's heat, and mid-time of the day,
To rest my limbs, upon a bed I lay;
One window shut, the other open stood,
Which gave such light as twinkles in a wood,
Like twilight glimpse at setting of the sun,
Or night being past, and yet not day begun;
Such light to shamefaced maidens must be shown
Where they may sport, and seem to be unknown:
Then came Corinna in her long loose gown,
Her white neck hid with tresses hanging down,
Resembling fair Semiramis going to bed,
Or Lais of a thousand wooers sped.
I snatched her gown being thin, the harm was small,
Yet strived she to be covered therewithal,
And striving thus as one that would be cast,
Betrayed herself, and yielded at the last.
Stark naked as she stood before mine eye,
Not one wen in her body could I spy.
What arms and shoulders did I touch and see,

How apt her breasts were to be pressed by me,
How smooth a belly under her waist saw I,
How large a leg, and what a lusty thigh.
To leave the rest, all liked me passing well;
I clinged her naked body, down she fell:
Judge you the rest, being tired she bade me kiss;
Jove send me more such afternoons as this!

(translated by Christopher Marlowe)

Petronius Arbiter

(d. 66 CE)

Doing, a Filthy Pleasure Is, and Short

DOING, a filthy pleasure is, and short;
And done, we straight repent us of the sport:
Let us not rush blindly on unto it;
Like lustful beasts, that only know to do it:
For lust will languish, and that heat decay.
But thus, thus, keeping endless holiday,
Let us together closely lie and kiss,
There is no labour, nor no shame in this;
This hath pleased, doth please, and long will please; never
Can this decay, but is beginning ever.

(translated by Ben Jonson)

Tzu Yeh

(4th century)

Busy in the Spring

BRIGHT moonlight shines through the trees.
In a rich brocade, the flowers bloom.

How can I not think of you—
alone, lonely, working at my loom.

A Smile

IN this house on a hill without walls,
the four winds touch our faces.

If they blow open your robe of gauze,
I'll try to hide my smile.

Song

WINTER skies are cold and low,
with harsh winds and freezing sleet.

But when we make love beneath our quilt,
we make three summer months of heat.

Agathias Scholasticus

(ca. 531–580)

BEAUTIFUL Melite, in the throes of middle age,
retains her youthful grace.
A blush on her cheek, she seduces
with her eyes. Many years have passed,
but not her girlish laughter.
All the ravages of time cannot overcome true nature.

Cometas Chartularius

(ca. 6th century)

PHYLLIS, loving Demophoön,
sent her eyes to sea.
But he, the fool,
had forgotten. And so he lied.

Now he lies alone upon the shore,
poor Demophoon,
and dreams of Phyllis who is gone,
and wonders why he cries.

Paulus Silentiarius

(d. ca. 575)

And there lay the lovers, lip-locked,
delirious, infinitely thirsting,

each wanting to go completely inside the other,
each filled to bursting with their love.

Like Achilles lying with Lycomedes,
her tunic pulled above her knees,

they grope and they fondle,
lips devouring lips, twisting like vines.

And he who is mine
trundles off to bed, thrice blessed.

He is mine in secret only—
we burn in separate beds.

COME, give me kisses, Rhodope,
and honor Holy Kypris.
But please, keep our love our secret—
the honeys of secret love taste sweetest.

TAKE off your clothes, my love!
Let's get naked! I want to feel you now.

Even your gauze dressing gown
feels thick as the walls of Babylon.

I want your lovely naked breast
against my naked breast.

Give me your lips.
Let the only veil be silence.

We are one.
Give me your tongue.

Even clothed in wrinkles, dear Philinna,
you are more beautiful than the young.

I'd sooner taste the apples
hanging heavy from your boughs

than pinch the firm breasts of girls.
I've no taste for the young.

Your autumn outshines a mortal spring,
your winter warmer than a summer sun.

Li Po

(701–762)

Women of Yueh

1

Southern women have alabaster skin,
and this one steers her boat for play.

Springtime dances in her eyes
when she picks water lilies
to give to romantic passersby.

2

Gathering lotuses by Yeh River,
she sings whenever someone passes,

then quickly hides her boat among the lilies—
so coy, pretending shyness.

3

Mirror Lake's waters are moon-clear,
and the woman from Yeh River

has a face pale as snow
that trembles in the ripples.

Blue Water

H E drifts on blue water
under a clear moon,
picking white lilies on South Lake.

Every lotus blossom
speaks of love
until his heart will break.

Resentment Near the Jade Steps

DEW whitens the jade steps.
This late, it soaks her gauze stockings.

She lowers her crystal blind to watch
the breaking, glass-clear moon of autumn.

Longing for Someone

LONGING for someone in Ch'ang-an—
crickets sing in autumn near the golden well.

Frosty winds bring a chill,
and my futon's the color of cold.

The lamp has burned low
and I am exhausted by longing.

I open the curtain to watch the moon,
but my sighs are all in vain.

She who is lovely as all the flowers
remains beyond the distant clouds.

The heavens are deep blue and endless;
below, the waves are pale.

The sky has no end, like my journey.
We suffer as we go.

Even dreams cannot cross over
the vast mountains that divide us.

And this eternal longing
can turn a heart to dust.

Otomo no Yakamochi

(718–785)

LATE evening finally comes:
I unlatch the door
and quietly await
the one
who greets me in my dreams.

WHEN my wife left home,
nothing at all could hold her.
Now she lies hidden
in the heart of the mountain
where my heart wanders alone.

Anonymous Chinese

(T'ang dynasty)

Lament

CHEEK by cheek on our pillows,
we promised to love until green mountains fall,

and iron floats on the river,
and the Yellow River itself runs dry;

to love till Orion rises in the day
and the north star wanders south.

We promised undying love until the sun
at midnight burns the sky.

Yuan Chen

(779–831)

Remembering

I DAYDREAM, melancholy at the windowsill—
memories I will never tell—

our passion in the late night hours,
our tearful goodbyes at dawn.

Mountains and rivers divide us,
I've given up hoping for rain.

Divided, I dream of you today—
I even embrace the pain.

Bamboo Mat

I CANNOT bear to put away
the bamboo sleeping-mat:

that night I brought you home,
I watched you roll it out.

Elegy

O LOVELIEST daughter of Hsieh,
you married a hapless scholar
and spent your life with a sewing basket,
patching his old clothes.

He thanked you
by selling your gold hairpins for wine;
he picked you herbs and berries
for your dinner
and locust leaves for the fire.

Now that they pay me handsomely,
there's no offering I can bring
but this sacrificial mourning.
We used to joke about dying.

And now you are suddenly gone.
I gave all your clothes away
and packed your needlework—
I couldn't bear to see them.

But I continue your kindness toward our maid,
and sometimes bring you gifts in my lonely dreams.
Everyone learns this sorrow, but none
more than those who suffer together.

Alone and lonely, I mourn us both.
Almost seventy, I know better men
who lived without a son, better poets
with dead wives who couldn't hear them.

In the dark of your tomb,
there is nothing left to hope for—
we had no faith in meeting after death.
Yet when I open my sleepless eyes,

I see through those long nights
the grief that troubled your life.

Empty House

I LEAVE my empty house at dawn
and ride to my empty office.

I fill the day with busywork;
at nightfall, back to my empty house.

Moonlight seeps through the cracks.
My wick is burnt to ash.

My heart lies cold in Hsien-yang Road
under the wheels of a hearse.

Li Ho

(791–817)

Melancholic

> She lies tonight
>   a thousand miles away,
> her night-black hair
>   spread out like all the heavens.
>
> Who was that shadow
>   lying there
> inside her shadow
>   until the candle vanished?
>
> The bamboo sleep-mat
>   I wove her
> is damp, pungent
>   with the sweat of all their passion.

Ariwara no Narihira

(825–880)

Is that the same moon?
Is this the same old springtime,
the same ancient spring?
And is this not my body,
the same body you once knew?

Li Hsun

(855–930)

To the Tune:

The Wine Spring

ETERNAL autumn rain—evening sounds
die out among the dying lotuses.

How can she bear to listen?
Wine has muddied her thinking.

And yet her thoughts continue like rain
after the candle has guttered,

after the incense burned.
—Almost at dawn,

when the misty rain is coldest,
it steals in through her screen.

To the Tune:

The Wine Spring

R AIN falls on fallen flowers
perfuming the edge of the pond
where she grieves through long separation.

When the song closes,
she closes her silver screen.

Night and day, sailboats leave for Ch'u.
In her pain, she tunes her lute.
The melody carries her grief,

and words vibrate in the strings,
words she cannot bear to sing.

Anonymous Japanese

(10th century)

> EARLY morning glows
> in the faint shimmer
> of first light.
> Choked with sadness,
> I help you into your clothes.

As night follows night,
I shift and turn my pillow,
my eyes open wide.
Long ago I dreamed of you.
How was I sleeping that night?

Ono no Komachi

(fl. mid–9th century)

> I LONG for him most
> during these long moonless nights.
> I lie awake, hot,
> the growing fires of passion
> bursting, blazing in my heart.

Izumi Shikibu

(970–1030)

> My black hair tangled
> as my own tangled thoughts,
> I lie here alone,
> dreaming of one who has gone,
> who stroked my hair till it shone.

WHEN I think of you,
fireflies in the marsh rise
like the soul's jewels,
lost to eternal longing,
abandoning my body

Liu Yung

(987–1053)

Song

SHE lowers her fragrant curtain,
wanting to speak her love.

She hesitates, she frowns—
the night is too soon over!

Her lover is first to bed,
warming the duck-down quilt.

She lays aside her needle,
drops her rich silk skirt,

eager for his embrace.
He asks one thing:

that the lamp remain lit.
He wants to see her face.

Samuel ha-Nagid

(993–1056)

I'D sell my soul for that fawn
of a boy   night walker
to sound of the 'ud & flute playing
who saw the glass in my hand   said
"drink the wine from between my lips"
& the moon was a *yod* drawn on
the cover of dawn—in gold ink

(translated by Jerome Rothenberg and
Harris Lenowitz)

THAT'S it—I love that fawn
plucking roses from
your garden—
you can put the blame on me
but if you once looked at my lover
with your eyes
your lovers would be hunting you
& you'd be gone
that boy who told me: pass
some honey from your hive
I answered: give me some back
on your tongue
& he got angry, yelled:
shall we two sin against the living God?
I answered: let your sin,
sweet master, be with me

(translated by Jerome Rothenberg and
Harris Lenowitz)

Ou-yang Hsiu

(1007–1072)

Faint Thunder Drifts beneath the Willow

FAINT thunder drifts . . .
                                beneath the willow,
rain upon the pool.
The sound of rain,
and rain again from lotus leaves.
The western eaves of this small place
cut through the rainbow.
I leaned on the rail and waited
for the moon to bloom.
A swallow flew and perched
                        to peer in at the ridgepole.
The moon, jade hook,
hung from the curtain rod.
No waves on water,
still waves, the wrinkles of the coverlet.
Behind the crystal screen, two pillows:
on one, a hairpin fell.

(translated by J. P. Seaton)

The Pool Is Full of Autumn Sky, Rippled by Gentle Breezes

THE pool is full of autumn sky, rippled by gentle
    breezes.
Strange misty skiff mounts on that sky,
and with the dew I pluck the lotus,
gift of autumn; on my heart,
the very flower marked with tears.

When you snap the lotus stalk,
the threads hang on.
Break the blossom off, stretch the threads:
draw out your heart.
As I sail home, I'll turn my glance
from lotus flowered margin of the waves:
from the shore, someone gazes.

(translated by J. P. Seaton)

Deep, Deep in the Shade of the Court

DEEP, deep in the shade of the court,
the oriole flutters and sings.
Sun warms, the mist warm; spring breathes heavily
again.
Green eyes, the willow leaves now turn toward
whom?
Across the distance, fragrant grass spreads out,
brooding, vacant, restlessly moving.

Wordless, she suffers, wounded that he'd go.
A shudder of love for him, and no way to show it.
She worries and worries, and finds her heart
unchanged:
over and over when she sleeps
the butterfly's imprisoned in her dreams.

(translated by J. P. Seaton)

Su Tung-p'o

(1037–1101)

Remembering My Wife

TEN years ago you died.
And my life ceased.
Even when I don't think of you,
I grieve. And with your grave
a thousand miles away,
there is no place for me
to give my grief a voice.
You wouldn't know me
if you saw me now,
me with snowy hair
and a dusty face.

I dreamed myself home
last night, and saw you
through a window
combing out your hair.
When you saw me,
we were speechless
till we burst into silent tears.

Year after year,
I recall that moonlit night
we spent alone together
among hills of stunted pine.

Li Ch'ing-chao

(1084–1151)

Plum Blossoms

THE fragrance of red lotuses has faded.
Autumn settles at my door.

I loosen my robe and drift in an orchid boat.
Someone sends me love notes in the clouds,

in lines of returning geese,
in moonlight filling the pavilion.

Flowers fade alone, rivers flow alone,
only our longing is shared.

Sadness, grief, worry—
weighing on my eyes,

we are so long apart—
settle in the bottom of my heart.

Spring at Wu Ling

THE breeze has passed,
pollen dust settled,
and now the evening comes
as I comb out my hair.

There is the book, the inkstone,
the table. But he who was
my life has disappeared.
It is hard to speak through tears.

I've heard it's always spring
at Wu Ling, and beautiful.
I'd take a little boat and drift
alone out on the water.

but I'm afraid a boat
so small would sink
with the weight
of all my sorrow.

Butterflies Love Flowers

WARM rains and gentle winds
have broken through the chill.
Willow eyes and peach buds
press on toward the sun.
I long for someone here
to share this poetry and wine.
But tears have streaked my rouge,
these silver phoenix pins
grow heavy in my hair.

In a gold-embroidered gown,
I hurl myself onto a mountain
made of downy pillows
and crush my favorite pins.
I hold myself in tired arms
until even my dreams turn black—
first dark, then black.
Deep in the deepening night,
I trim the lamp's black wick.

The Washing Stream

BEYOND barred windows,
shadows cover the garden,

shadows slide over the curtain
as I play my lute in silence.

Distant mountains stretch the sunset,
breezes bring clouds and rain.

The pear blossoms fade and die,
and I can't keep them from falling.

Boat of Stars

Spring after spring, I sat before my mirror.
Now I tire of braiding plum buds in my hair.

I've gone another year without you,
shuddering with each letter—

since you've gone,
even wine has lost its flavor.

I wept until it was autumn,
my thoughts going south beside you.

Even the Gates of Heaven
are nearer to me now than you.

Mahadeviyakka

(12th century)

On Her Decision to Stop Wearing Clothes

Coins in the hand
Can be stolen,
But who can rob this body
Of its own treasure?

The last thread of clothing
Can be stripped away,
But who can peel off Emptiness,
That nakedness covering all?

Fools, while I dress
In the Jasmine Lord's morning light,
I cannot be shamed—
What would you have me hide under silk
And the glitter of jewels?

(version by Jane Hirshfield)

Jelaluddin Rumi

(1207–1273)

Like This

IF anyone asks you
how the perfect satisfaction
of all our sexual wanting
will look, lift your face
and say,
> Like this.

When someone mentions the gracefulness
of the nightsky, climb up on the roof
and dance and say,
> Like this?

If anyone wants to know what "spirit" is,
or what "God's fragrance" means,
lean your head toward him or her.
Keep your face there close.
> Like this.

When someone quotes the old poetic image
about clouds gradually uncovering the moon,

slowly loosen knot by knot the strings
of your robe.
>   *Like this?*

If anyone wonders how Jesus raised the dead,
don't try to explain the miracle.
Kiss me on the lips.
>   *Like this. Like this.*

When someone asks what it means
to "die for love," point:
>   *here.*

If someone asks how tall I am, frown
and measure with your fingers the space
between the creases on your forehead.
>   *This tall.*

The soul sometimes leaves the body, then returns.
When someone doesn't believe that,
walk back into my house.
>   *Like this.*

When lovers moan,
they're telling our story.
>   *Like this.*

I am a sky where spirits live.
Stare into this deepening blue,
while the breeze says a secret.
>   *Like this.*

When someone asks what there is to do,
light the candle in his hand.

Like this.

How did Joseph's scent come to Jacob?

Huuuu.

How did Jacob's sight return?

Huuuuu.

A little wind cleans the eyes.
Like this.

When Shams comes back from Tabriz,
he'll put just his head around the edge
of the door to surprise us.

Like this.

(*translated by Coleman Barks*)

Shams was Rumi's beloved spiritual master.

You that love Lovers,
this is your home. Welcome!

In the midst of making form, Love
made this form that melts form,
with love for the door, and
Soul, the vestibule.

Watch the dust grains moving
in the light near the window.

Their dance is our dance.

We rarely hear the inward music,
but we're all dancing to it nevertheless,

directed by Shams,
the pure joy of the sun,
our Music Master.

(translated by Coleman Barks)

WHEN I see Your Face, the stones start spinning!
You appear; all studying wanders.
I lose my place.

Water turns pearly.
Fire dies down and doesn't destroy.

In Your Presence I don't want what I thought
I wanted, those three little hanging lamps.

Inside Your Face the ancient manuscripts
seem like rusty mirrors.

You breathe; new shapes appear,
and the music of a Desire as widespread
as Spring begins to move
like a great wagon.
                    Drive slowly.
Some of us walking alongside
are lame!

(translated by Coleman Barks)

WHAT I want is to see your face
    in a tree, in the sun coming out,
        in the air.

What I want is
    to hear the falcon-drum, and light again
        on your forearm.

You say, "Tell him I'm not here." The sound
    of that brusque dismissal
        becomes what I want.

To see in every palm your elegant silver coin-shavings,
    to turn with the wheel of the rain,
        to fall with the falling bread

of every experience,
    to swim like a huge fish
        in ocean water,

to be Jacob recognizing Joseph.
    To be a desert mountain
        instead of a city.

I'm tired of cowards.
    I want to live with lions.
        With Moses.

Not whining, teary people. I want
 the ranting of drunkards.
  I want to sing like birds sing,

not worrying who hears,
 or what they think.
  Last night,

a great teacher went from door to door
 with a lamp. "He who is not to be found
  is the one I'm looking for."

Beyond wanting, beyond place, inside form,
 That One. A flute says, *I have no hope*
  for finding that.

But Love plays
 and is the music played.
  Let that musician
finish this poem. Shams,
 I am a waterbird
  flying into the sun.

      (translated by Coleman Barks)

Hsu Tsai-ssu

(ca. 1300)

On Love

I'VE been loveless all my life,
but now that love is mine,
it drives me mad.

A body light as clouds,
a trembling willow heart—
my soul itself grows gossamer thin.

Perfume loses all its magic
waiting for a wandering friend,
and heartache comes in its time:

Whenever the lamp is low,
whenever the moon faintly shines.

Francesco Petrarch

(1304–1374)

IF constancy in love, if a brave heart,
the honeys of longing and courteous
desire, if passion built a gentle fire
somewhere in its winding labyrinth;

if my every thought was etched upon
my face, understood in broken words
or shattered by fear and shame, or if a
pallor, like a violet's, stained by love . . .

if love is to be altruistic,
if repeated sighs and weeping tears
feed equally on sorrow and rage;

if to burn at a distance or freeze
nearby, if love should dismantle me,
the blame is yours, Love, the loss with me.

Love delivers to me its sweetest thoughts
like a long forgotten confidant
telling me I was never so close
to what I have longed for as I am now.

I, who have believed and disbelieved,
can do no more than question now:
I live somewhere between the two,
my heart alternating yes and no.

And all the while, time quickly passes,
and my face in the mirror enters
a hopeless, contrary season.

Whatever comes, I do not age alone.
Desire remains unchanged.
What's left of my life grows brief.

Ikkyu Sojun

(1394–1481)

Face to Face with My Lover on
Daito's Anniversary

Monks recite the sutras in honor of the Founder,
their many voices cacophonous in my ear.
Afterward, making love, our intimate whispers
mock the empty formal discipline of others.

Song of the Dream Garden

PILLOWED on your thighs in a dream garden,
little flower with its perfumed stamen,
singing, sipping from the stream of you—
sunset, moonlight—our song continues.

My Hand Is Lady Mori's Hand

MY hand is Lady Mori's hand
and knows her mastery of love.
When I am weak, she resurrects my jeweled stem.
The monks I train are grateful then.

Night Talk in a Dream Chamber

Whether by sea or river or in mountains,
a monk in the world abandons fame and fortune.
Every night, we nestle like ducks in bed, sharing
intimate whispers, our bodies become at one.

My Love's Dark Place Is Fragrant
Like Narcissus

At midnight, your face in a dream brings a sigh.
Ch'u's love pavilion was long ago and far away.
But like a blossom on the flowering plum,
sweet narcissus blooms between your thighs.

Elegy

WE first lay down among flowers
ten years ago and found a timeless rapture.
Sadly, I remember being pillowed by her lap,
all-night love, all eternity in our vows.

Kabir

(1398–1448)

GIVE up erotic games, Kabir,
let longing flood your heart.
Only through tears of longing
can you glimpse the face of the beloved.

Sometimes, everywhere I look,
O my love, I see your radiant face.
With you ever present,
how could I close my eyes to anything?

Vidyapati

(15th century)

First Love

THE new moon stirs pangs of love.
Scratches mar her proud young breasts.
Often hidden, sometimes they lie revealed
like treasure in the hands of the poor.
Now she has known first love,
desires flood her mind,
she trembles with delight.
Safe from the eyes of gossipy friends,
she studies her reflection in a jewel,
knits her brow, and oh
so tenderly
touches the blossoming
love-bite on her lip.

Mirabai

(1498–1550)

Dark One,
all I request is a portion of love.
Whatever my defects,
you are for me an ocean of raptures.
Let the world cast its judgments
nothing changes my heart—
a single word from your lips is sufficient—
birth after birth
begging a share of that love.
Mira says: Dark One—enter the penetralia,
you've taken
this girl past the limits.

(translated by Andrew Schelling)

Don't block my way, friend—
I'm joining the sadhus.
The Dark One's image sits in my heart,
now nothing gives solace.
Oh the citizens sleep,
their world groggy with
ignorance,
but I hold vigils all night—
who understands these dark passions?
Wet with Shyam's love,
how could I sleep?
When it rains,
does anyone drink from the gutter?
Mira says: Friend—
take this lost child.
At midnight she goes out half mad
to slake her thirst
            at his fountain.

(translated by Andrew Schelling)

Shyam and *Dark One* are both epithets of Krishna.

HAVING wet me with love,
why did you leave?
You abandoned your unwavering consort,
having ignited her lamp wick;
she's like a pleasure boat
set out to drift on an ocean of craving.
Either way Mira's dead—
    unless you return.

(*translated by Andrew Schelling*)

A GLIMPSE of your body
has hooked me!
My family sets out to restrain me
but I'll never forget
how that peacock-plumed dancer embraced me.
I'm loggy with Shyam,
my people say—she meanders!
Yes Mira's hooked,
she goes for refuge into those deeps
where every secret is known.

(translated by Andrew Schelling)

William Shakespeare

(1564–1616)

Sonnet CXXIX

THE expense of spirit in a waste of shame
Is lust in action; and, till action, lust
Is perjur'd, murderous, bloody, full of blame,
Savage, extreme, rude, cruel, and not to trust;
Enjoy'd, no sooner but despised straight;
Past reason hunted; and no sooner had,
Past reason hated, as swallowed bait
On purpose laid to make the taker mad:
Mad in pursuit, and in possession so;
Had, having, and in quest to have, extreme;
A bliss in proof,—and prov'd, a very woe;
Before, a joy propos'd; behind, a dream.
        And this the world well knows; yet none
            knows well
        To shun the heaven that leads men to this hell.

Bihari

(1595–1664)

As if to lift my babe-in-arms,
my brazen lover touched my breast
with just a fingertip.

WHEN I found her in the bathing pool,
my footstep startled her—she crouched
to hide her breasts and glanced about.
Seeing no one else, her smile was shy.

ALL day she studies her new
love-bite in the mirror,
examining, covering,
then revealing it again.

LOVELINESS beyond words,
        this woman dressed
in a sari to match her skin,
        those beautiful breasts
concealed and yet exposed.

Robert Herrick

(1591–1674)

Delight in Disorder

A sweet disorder in the dress
Kindles in clothes a wantonness:
A lawn about the shoulders thrown
Into a fine distraction,
An erring lace, which here and there
Enthralls the crimson stomacher,
A cuff neglectful, and thereby
Ribbands to flow confusedly,
A winning wave (deserving note)
In the tempestuous petticoat,
A careless shoe-string, in whose tie
I see a wild civility,
Do more bewitch me, than when art
Is too precise in every part.

Clothes Do but Cheat and Cozen Us

Away with silks, away with lawn,
I'll have no scenes or curtains drawn;
Give me my mistress as she is,
Dress'd in her nak't simplicities:
For as my heart, e'en so my eye
Is won with flesh, not drapery.

Upon the Nipples of Julia's Breast

Have ye beheld (with much delight)
A red rose peeping through a white?
Or else a cherry (double grac'd)
Within a lily? Centre plac'd?
Or ever mark'd the pretty beam,
A strawberry shows, half drown'd in cream?
Or seen rich rubies blushing through
A pure smooth pearl, and orient too?
So like this, nay all the rest,
Is each neat niplet of her breast.

To His Mistress

HELP me! help me! now I call
To my pretty witchcrafts all;
Old I am, and cannot do
That I was accustomed to.
Bring your magics, spells, and charms,
To enflesh my thighs and arms;
Is there no way to beget
In my limbs their former heat?
Aesop had, as poets feign,
Baths that made him young again:
Find that medicine, if you can,
For your dry, decrepit man
Who would fain his strength renew,
Were it but to pleasure you.

Anne Bradstreet

(1612–1672)

To My Dear and Loving Husband

IF ever two were one, then surely we.
If ever man were lov'd by wife, then thee;
If ever wife was happy in a man,
Compare with me ye women if you can.
I prize thy love more than whole Mines of gold,
Or all the riches that the East doth hold.
My love is such that Rivers cannot quench,
Nor ought but love from thee, give recompence.
Thy love is such I can no way repay,
The heavens reward thee manifold I pray.
Then while we live, in love let's so persever,
That when we live no more, we may live ever.

Se Praj

(17th century)

Your breasts will not fall.
Why clothe them with flowers?

Your folded arms are a wall,
love inviting me over.

Andrew Marvell

(1621–1678)

To His Coy Mistress

HAD we but world enough, and time,
This coyness, lady, were no crime.
We would sit down, and think which way
To walk, and pass our long love's day.
Thou by the Indian Ganges' side
Should'st rubies find: I by the tide
Of Humber would complain. I would
Love you ten years before the flood,
And you should, if you please, refuse
Till the conversion of the Jews.

My vegetable love should grow
Vaster than empires, and more slow;
An hundred years should go to praise
Thine eyes, and on thy forehead gaze;
Two hundred to adore each breast,
But thirty thousand to the rest;
An age at least to every part,
And the last age should show your heart;

For, lady, you deserve this state,
Nor would I love at lower rate.

But at my back I always hear
Time's wingéd chariot hurrying near;
And yonder all before us lie
Deserts of vast eternity.
Thy beauty shall no more be found,
Nor, in thy marble vault, shall sound
My echoing song: then worms shall try
Thy long-preserved virginity,
And your quaint honor turn to dust,
And into ashes all my lust;
The grave's a fine and private place,
But none, I think, do there embrace.

Now, therefore, while the youthful hue
Sits on thy skin like morning dew,
And while thy willing soul transpires
At every pore with instant fires,
Now let us sport us while we may,
And now, like amorous birds of prey,
Rather at once our time devour
Than languish in his slow-chapt power.
Let us roll all our strength and all
Our sweetness up into one ball,
And tear our pleasures with rough strife
Through the iron gates of life:
Thus, though we cannot make our sun
Stand still, yet we will make him run.

John Dryden

(1631–1700)

Song for a Girl

>YOUNG I am, and yet unskill'd
>How to make a lover yield;
>How to keep, or how to gain,
>When to love, and when to feign.
>
>Take me, take me, some of you,
>While I yet am young and true;
>Ere I can my soul disguise,
>Heave my breasts, and roll my eyes.
>
>Stay not till I learn the way,
>How to lie, and to betray:
>He that has my first, is blest,
>For I may deceive the rest.
>
>Could I find a blooming youth,
>Full of love, and full of truth,
>Brisk, and of a jaunty mien,
>I should long to be fifteen.

Sor Juana Inés de la Cruz
(1651–1695)

Which Contains a Fantasy Satisfied
with a Love Befitting It

Semblance of my elusive love, hold still—
image of a bewitchment fondly cherished,
lovely fiction that robs my heart of joy,
fair mirage that makes it joy to perish.

Since already my breast, like willing iron,
yields to the powerful magnet of your charms,
why must you so flatteringly allure me,
then slip away and cheat my eager arms?

Even so, you shan't boast, self-satisfied,
that your tyranny has triumphed over me,
evade as you will arms opening wide,

all but encircling your phantasmal form:
in vain shall you elude my fruitless clasp,
for fantasy holds you captive in its grasp.

(translated by Alan S. Trueblood)

Jonathan Swift

(1667–1745)

Oysters

> CHARMING Oysters I cry
> My Masters come buy,
> So plump and so fresh,
> So sweet is their Flesh,
>   No *Colchester* Oyster
>   Is sweeter and moyster,
>   Your Stomach they settle,
>   And rouse up your Mettle,
>   They'll make you a Dad
>   Of a Lass or a Lad;
>   And, Madam your Wife
>   They'll please to the Life;
> Be she barren, be she old,
> Be she Slut, or be she Scold,
> Eat my Oysters, and lye near her,
> She'll be fruitful, never fear her.

William Blake

(1757–1827)

from *Visions*

THE moment of desire! the moment of desire!
    the virgin
That pines for man shall awaken her womb to
    enormous joys
In the secret shadows of her chamber: the youth
    shut up from
The lustful joy shall forget to generate & create an
    amorous image
In the shadows of his curtains and in the folds of
    his silent pillow.
Are not these the places of religion, the rewards of
    continence,
The self enjoyings of self denial? why dost thou
    seek religion?
Is it because acts are not lovely that thou seekest
    solitude
Where the horrible darkness is impressed with
    reflections of desire?

The Question Answer'd

WHAT is it men in women do require?
The lineaments of Gratified Desire.
What is it women do in men require?
The lineaments of Gratified Desire.

John Keats

(1795–1821)

Sharing Eve's Apple

O BLUSH not so! O blush not so!
  Or I shall think you knowing;
And if you smile the blushing while,
  Then maidenheads are going.

There's a blush for won't, and a blush for shan't,
  And a blush for having done it:
There a blush for thought and a blush for naught,
  And a blush for just begun it.

O sigh not so! O sigh not so!
  For it sounds of Eve's sweet pippin;
By these loosen'd lips you have tasted the pips
  And fought in an amorous nipping.

Will you play once more at nice-cut-core,
  For it only will last our youth out,
And we have the prime of the kissing time,
  We have not one sweet tooth out.

There's a sigh for yes, and a sigh for no,
    And a sigh for "I can't bear it!"—
O what can be done, shall we stay or run?
    O cut the sweet apple and share it.

Anonymous Somali

(ca. 19th century)

Woman's Love Song

You are so elegant in your robes,
exquisite as a jewelled ring.

Will I ever meet a man like you
whom I have seen but once?

An old umbrella comes undone;
you are strong as woven iron.

You are poured from Nairobi gold,
the first light of dawn, the blazing sun.

Will I ever meet a man like you,
you whom I have seen just once?

Walt Whitman

(1819–1892)

from *I Sing the Body Electric*

THIS is the female form,
A divine nimbus exhales from it from head to foot,
It attracts with fierce undeniable attraction,
I am drawn by its breath as if I were no more than a
    helpless vapor, all falls aside but myself and it,
Books, art, religion, time, the visible and solid earth,
    and what was expected of heaven or fear'd of hell,
    are now consumed,
Mad filaments, ungovernable shoots play out of it,
    the response likewise ungovernable,
Hair, bosom, hips, bend of legs, negligent falling
    hands all diffused, mine too diffused,
Ebb stung by the flow and flow stung by the ebb,
    love-flesh swelling and deliciously aching,
Limitless limpid jets of love hot and enormous,
    quivering jelly of love, white-blow and delirious
    juice,
Bridegroom night of love working surely and softly
    into the prostrate dawn,

Undulating into the willing and yielding day,
Lost in the cleave of the clasping and sweet-flesh'd
day.

This the nucleus—after the child is born of woman,
man is born of woman,
This the bath of birth, this the merge of small and
large, and the outlet again.

Be not ashamed women, your privilege encloses the
rest, and is the exit of the rest,
You are the gates of the body, and you are the gates
of the soul.

The female contains all qualities and tempers
of them,
She is in her place and moves with perfect balance,
She is all things duly veil'd, she is both passive
and active,
She is to conceive daughters as well as sons, and
sons as well as daughters.

As I see my soul reflected in Nature,
As I see through a mist, One with inexpressible
completeness, sanity, beauty,
See the bent head and arms folded over the breast,
the Female I see.

from *I Sing the Body Electric*

THE male is not less the soul nor more, he too is in
his place,
He too is all qualities, he is action and power,
The flush of the known universe is in him,
Scorn becomes him well, and appetite and defiance
become him well,
The wildest largest passions, bliss that is utmost,
sorrow that is utmost become him well, pride is
for him,
The full-spread pride of man is calming and
excellent in the soul,
Knowledge becomes him, he likes it always, he
brings every thing to the test of himself,
Whatever the survey, whatever the sea and the sail,
he strikes soundings at last only here,
(Where else does he strike soundings except here?

The man's body is sacred and the woman's body
is sacred,
No matter who it is, it is sacred—is it the meanest
one in the laborers' gang?
Is it one of the dull-faced immigrants just landed on
the wharf?
Each belongs here or anywhere just as much as the

well-off, just as much as you,
Each has his or her place in the procession.

(All is a procession,
The universe is a procession with measured and
   perfect motion.)

Do you know so much yourself that you call the
   meanest ignorant?
Do you suppose you have a right to a good sight,
   and he or she has no right to a sight?
Do you think matter has cohered together from its
   diffuse float,
     and the soil is on the surface, and water runs and
     vegetation sprouts,

For you only, and not for him and her?

A Woman Waits for Me

A woman waits for me, she contains all, nothing
    is lacking,
Yet all were lacking if sex were lacking, or if the
    moisture
        of the right man were lacking.

Sex contains all, bodies, souls,
Meanings, proofs, purities, delicacies, results,
    promulgations,
Songs, commands, health, pride, the maternal
    mystery, the seminal milk,
All hopes, benefactions, bestowals, all the passions,
    loves, beauties, delights of the earth,
These are contain'd in sex as parts of itself and
    justifications of itself.

Without shame the man I like knows and avows the
    deliciousness of his sex,
Without shame the woman I like knows and
    avows hers.

Now I will dismiss myself from impassive women,
I will go stay with her who waits for me, and with
    those women
        that are warm-blooded and sufficient for me,

I see they understand me and do not deny me,
I see that they are worthy of me, I will be the robust
   husband of those women.

They are not one jot less than I am,
They are tann'd in the face by the shining suns and
   blowing winds,
Their flesh has the old divine suppleness and
   strength,
They know how to swim, row, ride, wrestle, shoot,
   run, strike,
   retreat, advance, rest, defend themselves,
They are ultimate in their own right—they are
   calm, clear,
well-possess'd of themselves.

I draw you close to me, you women,
I cannot let you go, I would do you good,
I am for you, and you are for me, not only for our
   own sake, but for others' sakes,
Envelop'd in you sleep greater heroes and bards,
They refuse to awake at the touch of any man
   but me.

It is I, you women, I make my way,
I am stern, acrid, large, undissuadable, but I love you,
I do not hurt you any more than is necessary
   for you,
I pour the stuff to start sons and daughters fit for
   these States,

I press with slow rude muscle,
I brace myself effectually, I listen to no entreaties,
I dare not withdraw till I deposit what has so long
     accumulated within me.

Through you I drain the pent-up rivers of myself,
In you I wrap a thousand onward years,
On you I graft the grafts of the best-beloved of me
     and America,
The drops I distil upon you shall grow fierce and
     athletic girls,
          new artists, musicians, and singers,
The babes I beget upon you are to beget babes in
     their turn,
I shall demand perfect men and women out of my
     love-spendings,
I shall expect them to interpenetrate with others,
     as I and you interpenetrate now,
I shall count on the fruits of the gushing showers
     of them,
          as I count on the fruits of the gushing showers I
          give now,
I shall look for loving crops from the birth, life,
     death, immortality,
          I plant so lovingly now.

I Am He That Aches with Love

I AM he that aches with amorous love;
Does the earth gravitate? does not all matter,
   aching, attract all matter?
So the body of me to all I meet or know.

City of Orgies

City of orgies, walks and joys,
City whom that I have liv'd and sung in your midst
    will one day make you illustrious,
Not the pageants of you, not your shining tableaus,
    your spectacles, repay me,
Not the interminable rows of your houses, nor the
    ships at the wharves,
Nor the processions in the streets, nor the bright
    windows with goods in them,
Nor to converse with learn'd persons, or bear my
    share in the soiree or feast;
Not those, but as I pass O Manhattan, your fre-
    quent and swift flash of eyes offering me love,
Offering response to my own—these repay me,
Lovers, continual lovers, only repay me.

Charles Baudelaire

(1821–1867)

Possessed

THE sun is in mourning. Be like the sun,
moon of my life, swathe yourself in crepe,
sleep, smoke, whatever—be still or glum,
plummet to the depths of boredom's pit—

I love you there. But if now your whim—
like the moon leaving her eclipse behind—
is to strut in the places where Folly throngs,
so be it! Lovely dagger, leave your sheath!

Light your eyes in the gaslamps' glow,
light others' with their lust for you . . .
Anything goes: sullen or submissive,

be what you will, black night, red dawn—
each nerve of my trembling body cries:
'Dear Demon, with this I thee worship!'

(translated by Richard Howard)

Anonymous Chinook

(ca. 1888)

I won't care
if you desert me.

There are many pretty boys in town.
Soon, I shall have another one.
It's easy to find another one.

Emily Dickinson

(1830–1886)

WILD Nights — Wild Nights!
Were I with thee
Wild Nights should be
Our luxury!

Futile — the Winds —
To a Heart in port —
Done with the Compass —
Done with the Chart!

Rowing in Eden —
Ah, the Sea!
Might I but moor — Tonight —
in Thee!

Anonymous Kwakiutl

(ca. 1896)

FIRES run through my body—the pain of loving you.
Pain runs through my body with the fires of my love
    for you.
Sickness wanders my body with my love for you.
Pain like a boil about to burst with my love for you.
Consumed by fire with my love for you.
I remember what you said to me.
I am thinking of your love for me.
I am torn by your love for me.

Pain and more pain.
Where are you going with my love?
I'm told you will go from here.
I am told you will leave me here.
My body is numb with grief.
Remember what I've said, my love.
Goodbye, my love, goodbye.

Anonymous Inuit

(ca. 1894–97)

Oxaitoq's Song

WALKING inland, inland, inland,
I am walking inland.

Nobody loves me, she least of all, so I walk inland.
She has loved me only for the things I bring.
She has loved me only for the food I bring.

Paul Laurence Dunbar

(1872–1906)

Passion and Love

A MAIDEN wept and, as a comforter,
Came one who cried, "I love thee," and he seized
Her in his arms and kissed her with hot breath,
That dried tears upon her flaming cheeks.
While evermore his boldly blazing eye
Burned into hers; but she uncomforted
Shrank from his arms and only wept the more.

Then one came and gazed mutely in her face
With wide and wistful eyes; but still aloof
He held himself; as with a reverent fear,
As one who knows some sacred presence nigh.
And as she wept he mingled tear with tear,
That cheered her soul like dew a dusty flower,—
Until she smiled, approached, and touched his hand!

Longing

IF you could sit with me beside the sea to-day,
And whisper with me sweetest dreamings o'er
   and o'er;
I think I should not find the clouds so dim and gray,
And not so loud the waves complaining at the
   shore.

If you could sit with me upon the shore to-day,
And hold my hand in yours as in the days of old,
I think I should not mind the chill baptismal spray,
Nor find my hand and heart and all the world
   so cold.

If you could walk with me upon the strand to-day,
And tell me that my longing love had won your own,
I think all my sad thoughts would then be put away,
And I could give back laughter for the Ocean's moan!

Antonio Machado

(1875–1939)

Iғ I were a poet
of love, I would make
a poem for your eyes as clear
as the transparent water in the marble pool.

And in my water poem
this is what I would say:

"I know your eyes do not answer mine,
they look and do not question when they look:
your clear eyes, your eyes have
the calm and good light,
the good light of the blossoming world that I saw
one day from the arms of my mother."

(translated by Robert Bly)

Yosano Akiko

(1878–1942)

S<small>PRING</small> quickly passes,
everything perishes.
I cry out loud
whenever your touches
tingle my breasts.

A THOUSAND strands
of glistening deep black hair
in tangles, tangles,
all intertangled
like my dreams of you.

ARE you still longing,
seeking what is beautiful,
what is decent and true?
Here in my hand, this flower,
my love, is shockingly red.

Anna Akhmatova

(1889–1966)

The Guest

NOTHING is changed: against the dining-room
    windows
hard grains of whirling snow still beat.
I am what I was,
but a man came to me.

"What do you want?" I asked.
"To be with you in hell," he said.
I laughed, "It's plain you mean
to have us both destroyed."

He lifted his thin hand
and lightly stroked the flowers:
"Tell me how men kiss you,
tell me how you kiss."

His torpid eyes were fixed
unblinking on my ring.
Not a single muscle stirred
in his clear, sardonic face.

Oh, I see: his game is that he knows
intimately, ardently,
there's nothing from me he wants,
I have nothing to refuse.

*(translated by Stanley Kunitz
with Max Hayward)*

Federico García-Lorca

(1898–1936)

The Unfaithful Wife

AND so I led her down to the river,
thinking her unwed,
but she already had a husband.
It was St. James' night
and almost a foregone conclusion.
The streetlight went out
and the crickets came on.
In the farthest streets,
I touched her sleeping breasts,
and they opened to me suddenly
like fronds of hyacinth,
her starched petticoat
sounded to my ears
like a piece of silk
shredded by ten knives.
Silver light vanished from their leaves,
the trees have grown larger,
and the dogs of dawn's horizon
barked far beyond the river.

Past blackberry brambles,
past hawthorn and reeds,
under her heavy hair,
I made a hollow in the earth.
I took off my tie.
She slipped off her dress.
I took off my pistol belt;
she, four bodices.
No fragrant oil or mother of pearl
could match her fine smooth skin,
nor moonlit crystal glass
or mirror glow so bright.
Her thighs eluded me
like frightened fish
half filled with fire,
half filled with ice.
The road I ran that night
can't be compared—
no bridle, no stirrup,
I rode a pearl mare.
Being a man, I can't repeat
all the things she said—
The light of knowledge
demands I be discreet.
Stained with sand and kisses,
I took her from the river.
Lilies raised their swords
to pierce the passing breeze.

I behaved like what I am.
Like a legitimate gypsy.
I gave her a big sewing basket
lined with straw-colored satin,
and I did not fall in love,
because, despite a husband at home,
she told me she was unmarried
when I led her down to the river.

Pablo Neruda

(1904–1973)

Body of a Woman

Body of a woman, white hills, white thighs,
you look like a world, lying in surrender.
My rough peasant's body digs in you
and makes the son leap from the depth of the earth.

I was alone like a tunnel. The birds fled from me,
and night swamped me with its crushing invasion.
To survive myself I forged you like a weapon,
like an arrow in my bow, a stone in my sling.

But the hour of vengeance falls, and I love you.
Body of skin, of moss, of eager and firm milk.
Oh the goblets of the breast! Oh the eyes of absence!
Oh the roses of the pubis! Of your voice, slow
    and sad!

Body of my woman, I will persist in your grace.
My thirst, my boundless desire, my shifting road!
Dark river-beds where the eternal thirst flows
and weariness follows, and the infinite ache.

(translated by W. S. Merwin)

Love Song

I LOVE you, I love you, is my song
and here my silliness begins.

I love you, I love you my lung,
I love you, I love you my wild grapevine,
and if love is like wine:
you are my predilection
from your hands to your feet:
you are the wineglass of hereafter
and my bottle of destiny.

I love you forwards and backwards,
and I don't have the tone or the timbre
to sing you my song,
my endless song.

On my violin that sings out of tune
my violin declares,
I love you, I love you my double bass,
my sweet woman, dark and clear,
my heart, my teeth,
my light and my spoon,
my salt of the dim week,
my clear windowpane moon.

(translated by William O'Daly)

Kenneth Rexroth

(1905–1982)

Sottoportico San Zaccaria

I⊤ rains on the roofs
As it rains in my poems
Under the thunder
We fit together like parts
Of a magic puzzle
Twelve winds beat the gulls from the sky
And tear the curtains
And lightning glisters
On your sweating breasts
Your face topples into dark
And the wind sounds like an army
Breaking through dry reeds
We spread our aching bodies in the window
And I can smell the odor of hay
In the female smell of Venice

Quietly

LYING here quietly beside you,
My cheek against your firm, quiet thighs,
The calm music of Boccherini
Washing over us in the quiet,
As the sun leaves the housetops and goes
Out over the Pacific, quiet—
So quiet the sun moves beyond us,
So quiet as the sun always goes,
So quiet, our bodies, worn with the
Times and the penances of love, our
Brains curled, quiet in their shells, dormant,
Our hearts slow, quiet, reliable
In their interlocked rhythms, the pulse
In your thigh caressing my cheek. Quiet.

Sa'id 'Aql
(b. 1912)

More Beautiful than Your Eyes

MORE beautiful than your eyes is my love
for your eyes. When you sing, all being sings.

Are you there above me, star of my longing,
or are you just a phantom dream?

When I think of you, fragrances enter me—
Can it be you were created by a rose?

Perhaps the longing for beauty made you,
raised and hopeful hands designed your form.

Do the strings of the passionately fingered lute
imagine those who yearn for melody?

We meet in moments truant from time,
free from boundaries, dissolving all bounds.

The beckoning universe swings us into the heavens
on an endless flight.

The most beautiful aspect of our land
is the vision that you have lived here.

> (*translated by Matthew Sorenson and
> Naomi Shihab Nye*)

Thomas McGrath

(1916–1990)

A Coal Fire in Winter

Something old and tyrannical burning there.
(Not like a wood fire which is only
The end of a summer, or a life)
But something of darkness: heat
From the time before there was fire.
And I have come here
To warm that blackness into forms of light,
To set free a captive prince
From the sunken kingdom of the father coal.

A warming company of the cold-blooded—
These carbon serpents of bituminous gardens,
These inflammable tunnels of dead song from the
    black pit,
This sparkling end of the great beasts, these blazing
Stone flowers diamond fire incandescent fruit.
And out of all that death, now,
At midnight, my love and I are riding
Down the old high roads of inexhaustible light.

Hayden Carruth
(b. 1921)

Two Sonnets

I

To see a woman long oppressed by fear
come free at last is joyous and a wonder.
As a poet I don't care for the stale remainder
of conventional sonnetry, yet just to savor
my own outpouring pleasure in this affair
I must lean backward lazily, as it were,
in the old romantic bed, an absconder
and apostate in my era. Today I wonder
where love's ideas lead me, and I don't care.

Well, she is like a *flower*. Let's say a Turk's-cap
        lily. Somehow the nodding horn has lifted
and its complex hazel smile has opened
to the light. More, more, it has *wafted*
a clear high tone like a trumpet from the steppe
of home to heaven, that there has never happened.

2

You rose from our embrace and the small light
    spread
like an aureole around you. The long parabola
of neck and shoulder, flank and thigh I saw
permute itself through unfolding and unlimited
minuteness in the movement of your tall tread,
the spine-root swaying, the Picasso-like éclat
of scissoring slender legs. I knew some law
of Being was at work. At one time I had said
that love bestows such values, and so it does,
but the old man in his canto was right and wise:
ubi amor ibi ocullus est.
Always I wanted to give and in wanting was
the poet. A man now, aging, I know the best
of love is not to bestow, but to recognize.

Denise Levertov

(b. 1923)

Our Bodies

Our bodies, still young under
the engraved anxiety of our
faces, and innocently

more expressive than faces:
nipples, navel, and pubic hair
make anyway a

sort of face: or taking
the rounded shadows at
breast, buttock, balls,

the plump of my belly, the
hollow of your
groin, as a constellation,

how it leans from earth to
dawn in a gesture of
play and

wise compassion—
nothing like this

comes to pass
in eyes or wistful
mouths.
       I have

a line or groove I love
runs down
my body from breastbone
to waist. It speaks of
eagerness, of
distance.

       Your long back,
the sand color and
how the bones show, say

what sky after sunset
almost white
over a deep woods to which

rooks are homing, says.

The Mutes

THOSE groans men use
passing a woman on the street
or on the steps of the subway

to tell her she is a female
and their flesh knows it,

are they a sort of tune,
an ugly enough song, sung
by a bird with a slit tongue

but meant for music?

Or are they the muffled roaring
of deafmutes trapped in a building that is
slowly filling with smoke?

Perhaps both.

Such men most often
look as if groan were all they could do,
yet a woman, in spite of herself,

knows it's a tribute:
if she were lacking all grace
they'd pass her in silence:

so it's not only to say she's
a warm hole. It's a word

in grief-language, nothing to do with
primitive, not an ur-language;
language stricken, sickened, cast down

in decrepitude. She wants to
throw the tribute away, dis-
gusted, and can't,

it goes on buzzing in her ear,
it changes the pace of her walk,
the torn posters in echoing corridors

spell it out, it
quakes and gnashes as the train comes in.
Her pulse sullenly

had picked up speed,
but the cars slow down and
jar to a stop while her understanding

keeps on translating:
'Life after life after life goes by

without poetry,
without seemliness,
without love.'

Carolyn Kizer

(b. 1925)

The Glass

Your body tolls the hour,
The hands spin round and round.
Your face, the focus of light,
Will burn me to the ground.

Losing ourselves in Love
Beneath this counterpane,
Unwinding from its womb
To the all-consuming now,

All day today I die,
I die eternally,
Losing myself in joy.
By one touch you put out time.

Robert Creeley

(b. 1926)

A Form of Women

I HAVE come far enough
from where I was not before
to have seen the things
looking in at me through the open door

and have walked tonight
by myself
to see the moonlight
and see it as trees

and shapes more fearful
because I feared
what I did not know
but have wanted to know.

My face is my own, I thought.
But you have seen it
turn into a thousand years.
I watched you cry.

I could not touch you.
I wanted very much to

touch you
but could not.

If it is dark
when this is given to you,
have care for its content
when the moon shines.

My face is my own.
My hands are my own.
My mouth is my own
but I am not.

Moon, moon,
when you leave me alone
all the darkness is
an utter blackness,

a pit of fear,
a stench,
hands unreasonable
never to touch.

But I love you.
Do you love me.
What to say
when you see me.

The Rain

A<small>LL</small> night the sound had
come back again,
and again falls
this quiet, persistent rain.

What am I to myself
that must be remembered,
insisted upon
so often? Is it

that never the ease,
even the hardness,
of rain falling
will have for me

something other than this,
something not so insistent—
am I to be locked in this
final uneasiness.

Love, if you love me,
lie next to me.
Be for me, like rain,
the getting out

of the tiredness, the fatuousness, the semi-
lust of intentional indifference.
Be wet
with a decent happiness.

Adrienne Rich

(b. 1929)

from *Twenty-one Love Poems*

I WAKE up in your bed. I know I have been dreaming.
Much earlier, the alarm broke us from each other,
you've been at your desk for hours. I know what I
    dreamed:
our friend the poet comes into my room
where I've been writing for days,
drafts, carbons, poems are scattered everywhere,
and I want to show her one poem
which is the poem of my life. But I hesitate,
and wake. You've kissed my hair
to wake me. *I dreamed you were a poem,*
I say, *a poem I wanted to show someone . . .*
and I laugh and fall dreaming again
of the desire to show you to everyone I love,
to move openly together
in the pull of gravity, which is not simple,
which carries the feathered grass a long way down
    the upbreathing air.

Roberto Sosa

(b. 1930)

The Most Ancient Names of Fire

BLESSED are the lovers
for theirs is the grain of sand
that sustains the center of the seas.

Dazed by the play of fountains
they hear nothing
but the music sprinkled by their names.

Trembling
they cling to one another
like small frightened animals who tremble, knowing
    they will die.

Nothing is alien to them.

Their only strength against the wind and tide
are the beautifying words of all existence: I love you.
We shall grow old together to the end.

Male and female ravens steal lovers' eyes,
their beautiful gestures, even the moon in their
    mirror
but not the fire
from which they are reborn.

(translated by Jo Anne Engelbert)

Robert Kelly

(b. 1935)

Poem for Easter

ALL women are beautiful as they rise
exultant from the ruins they make of us

& this woman
who lies back informing the sheets

has slain me with all day love & now
keeps vigil at the tomb of my desire

from which also she will make me rise
& come before her into galilee

Rising I fall
& what does her beauty matter

except it is a darkness sabbath
where the church—our bodies

everywhere come together—
kindles one small light

from the unyielding the flint
then resurrection

The radio Messiah
I know

that my redeemer liveth
& he shall stand in the last days

up from this earth
beyond blasphemy

beyond misunderstanding
O love this hour will not let me name

they will say I make
a sexual mystery of your passion

whereas we know
flesh rises

to apprehend one other mystery
as the lover's

astonished eyes come open in his coming
to find that he is not alone

Lucille Clifton
(b. 1936)

the women you are accustomed to

> wearing that same black dress,
> their lips and asses tight,
> their bronzed hair set in perfect place;
> these women gathered in my dream
> to talk their usual talk,
> their conversation spiked with the names
> of avenues in France.

> and when i asked them what the hell,
> they shook their marble heads
> and walked erect out of my sleep,
> back into a town which knows
> all there is to know
> about the cold outside, while i relaxed
> and thought of you,
> your burning blood, your dancing tongue

song at midnight

> *. . . do not*
> *send me out*
> *among strangers*
> *   —Sonia Sanchez*

brothers,
this big woman
carries much sweetness
in the folds of her flesh.
her hair
is white with wonderful.
she is
rounder than the moon
and far more faithful.
brothers,
who will hold her,
who will find her beautiful
if you do not?

won't you celebrate with me
what I have shaped into
a kind of life? i had no model.
born in babylon

both nonwhite and woman
what did i see to be except myself?
i made it up
here on this bridge between
starshine and clay,
my one hand holding tight
my other hand; come celebrate
with me that everyday
something has tried to kill me
and has failed.

Jaan Kaplinski
(b. 1941)

NIGHT comes and extinguishes the numbers and
    the year
lifts us from the past and brings away
from the checkerboard table from among kings
    queens and knights
the wind's silence and the source the seventh
    witness
which is a tiny beginning, roots, our infinite roots
wakening still sleeping still in stone crevices in soil
without knowing oneself even without understanding
    who he is who is woven into them
through the dark earth thus the trees meet all at
    once in the upper and lower world through
    mother's mute flesh
fingers with fingers, leaves with leaves, loins with
    loins,
silently blood and earth fall from between us
your young body bursts into flames under dry leaves

Sam Hamill
(b. 1943)

Ten Thousand Sutras
(after Hakuin)

THE body is the body of the Buddha.
Like ice and water, the one is always in the other.

In the middle of the lake
we long for a drink of water.

Adrift in Samsara
we dream of blissful Nirvana.

This body is the body of the Buddha,
this moment an eternity.

Saying *I love you,* the deed is done—
the name and the deed are one.

With you and without you
the line runs straight—

your body is the body of the Buddha,
there is light beyond the gate.

This love I give to you
is the love that comes from Kannon.

Every breath a sutra.
Going or returning, it's the same.

Our bodies are the bodies of the Buddha,
our names are Kannon's name.

No word can adequately say it,
yet every word must praise it—

in silent meditation
destroying evil karma,

in silent meditation
inhabiting the Dharma—

this body is the body of the Buddha,
your body is the body of the Buddha.

Open arms and eyes to Samsara!
Embraced by the thousand arms of Kannon!

In the perfect mind of *vivikta-dharma,*
the truth of solitude,

our body is a temple,
not a refuge.

Praise our body
even in Samsara,

our bodies are the body of the Buddha,
our bodies are the body of the Buddha.

Gioconda Belli

(b. 1948)

from *Brief Lessons in Eroticism I*

I

To sail the entire length of a body
Is to circle the world
To navigate the rose of the winds without a compass
Islands gulfs peninsulas breakwaters against crash-
    ing waves
It's not easy to find such pleasure
Don't think you can get it in one day or night of
    consoling sheets
There are enough secrets in the pores to fill many
    moons

II

The body is an astral chart in a coded language
Find a star and perhaps you'll begin
To change course when suddenly a hurricane or
    piercing scream
Makes you tremble in fear
A crease in the hand you didn't expect

III

Go over the entire length many times
Find the lake with white water lilies
Caress the lily's center with your anchor
Plunge deep drown yourself stretch your limbs
Don't deny yourself the smell the salt the sugar
The heavy winds cumulonimbus-lungs
The brain's dense fog
Earthquake of legs
Sleeping tidal waves of kisses

IV

Place yourself in the humus without fear
of wearing out there's no hurry
Delay reaching the peak
the threshold of paradise
Rock your fallen angel let your ursurped sword of fire
lose itself in the thick hair
Bite the apple

VI

Listen to the shell of the ear
How the dampness moans
Earlobe approaching the lip sound of breathing
Pores that rise up to form tiny mountains
Shivery insurrection of skin caressed
Gentle bridge neck go down to the sea breast
The heart's tide whisper to her
Find the grotto of water.

VIII

Breathe in breathe out
Die a little
Sweetly slowly die
Come to death against the eye's center let the
    pleasure go on
Turn the rudder spread the sails
Sail on toward Venus
morning star
—the sea like a vast mercuric crystal—
sleep you shipwrecked sailor.

(translated by Steven White)

Olga Broumas

(b. 1949)

For Every Heart

I LIKE it when my friend has lovers, their happy
  moans,
unrestrained, fill the house with the glee of her
  prowess.
As in China, during the concert of the laser harp,
cameras added their applause, percussive,
while the umbilical fanned neon from each note
in the open-air theater and ribboned the path of
  stars,
I am moved to clap. Hands clapping calm us.
It is their simple, wholehearted and naive sexual
  imitation
their fleshbird dance chest-high in the open of time.

Perpetua

> As the seed of a mole for
> Generations carried across
> Time on a woman's belly
> Flowers one morning blackly
> Exposed to poison and poison
> Itself is not
> Disease but mutation is one
> Understanding the strong
> Shaft of your clitoris I kiss
> As the exposed tip of your
> Heart is another

Maurya Simon
(b. 1950)

Shiva's Prowess

THERE are ecstatic rituals every do-good deity
    knows;
there are myriad ways to flout, grin, and pose,

so that even virgins undulate like struck water—
but no one, states the Puranas, will ever master

a fraction of the multi-million postures shiva savors.
His sacred prowess is cause for my wonder—

coming from a god who smells like burnt grass,
who wears two cobras coiled around his biceps—

what strange fires must smoulder beneath his skin,
and what an appetite to quench, when he is
    smitten;

for he's a being whose gaze unleashes rivers, an
    ocean
of desire, a lover whose smile's a danger zone,

whose touch awakens sunken leviathans to rise
up like fountains from their former lives.

Eight million ways to move, make love, to take
a woman out of her body and soul, and bring her
   back—

postures whirling like tornados, brief as eclipses,
ceremonial as a rain dance; movements slick

as oiled arias; kisses inspiring drugged trances:
his tongue a glistening shrine, his teeth avalanches,

his mouth hewn from the deepest hole in space,
his breath a meadow of mint, a web of spindrift,

his wide neck taut with cords of rolling muscles,
his chest an orchestra, his heart a ship's hull,

his arms huge sea nets, opposing shores,
his belly an island forested in ripe mangoes,

his penis a gourd into which the universe flows,
and his entry like the moment of death—

Dorianna Laux

(b. 1952)

The Lovers

S HE is about to come. This time,
they are sitting up, joined below the belly,
feet cupped like sleek hands praying
at the base of each other's spines.
And when something lifts within her
toward a light she's sure, once again,
she can't bear, she opens her eyes
and sees his face is turned away,
one arm behind him, hand splayed
palm down on the mattress, to brace himself
so he can lever his hips, touch
with the bright tip the innermost spot.
And she finds she *can't* bear it—
not his beautiful neck, stretched and corded,
not his hair fallen to one side like beach grass,
not the curved wing of his ear, washed thin
with daylight, deep pink of the inner body—
What she can't bear is that she can't see his face,
not that she thinks this exactly—she is rocking

and breathing—it's more her body's thought,
opening, as it is, into its own sheer truth.
So that when her hand lifts of its own volition
and slaps him, twice on the chest,
on that pad of muscled flesh just above the nipple,
slaps him twice, fast, like a nursing child
trying to get a mother's attention,
she's startled by the sound,
though when he turns his face to hers—
which is what her body wants, his eyes
pulled open, as if she had bitten—
she does reach out and bite him, on the shoulder,
not hard, but with the power infants have
over those who have borne them, tied as they are
to the body, and so, tied to the pleasure,
the exquisite pain of this world.
And when she lifts her face he sees
where she's gone, knows she can't speak,
is traveling toward something essential,
toward the core of her need, so he simply
watches, steadily, with an animal calm
as she arches and screams, watches the face that,
if she could see it, she would never let him see.

The Thief

WHAT is it when your man sits on the floor
in sweatpants, his latest project
set out in front of him like a small world, maps
and photographs, diagrams and plans, everything
he hopes to build, invent or create,
and you believe in him as you always have,
even after the failures, even more now
as you set your coffee down
and move toward him, to where he sits
oblivious to you, concentrating
in a square of sun—
you step over the rulers and blue graph paper
to squat behind him, and he barely notices
though you're still in your robe
which falls open a little as you reach
around his chest, feel for the pink
wheel of each nipple, the slow beat
of his heart, your ear pressed to his back
to listen—and you are torn,
not wanting to interrupt his work
but unable to keep your fingers
from dipping into the ditch of his pants,
torn again with tenderness
for the way his flesh grows unwillingly

toward your curved palm, toward the light,
as if you had planted it, this sweet root,
your mouth already an echo of its shape—
you slip your tongue into his ear
and he hears you, calling him away
from his work, the angled lines of his thoughts,
into the shapeless place you are bound
to take him, over bridges of bone, beyond
borders of skin, climbing over him
into the world of the body, its labyrinth
of ladders and stairs—and you love him
like the first time you loved him,
with equal measures of expectancy
and fear and awe, taking him with you
into the soft geometry of the flesh, the earth
before its sidewalks and cities,
its glistening spires,
stealing him back from the world he loves
into this other world he cannot build without you.

NOTES ON THE POETS

Poets are listed here in order of appearance.

SAPPHO was born in the late-seventh century BCE on the Greek island of Lesbos (from which we derive *lesbian* because of Sappho's fame). Only one of her poems exists in its entirety; the rest only survives in fragments. She is best known for her passionate lyrics and for the cult that grew around her. She is said to have drowned, leaping from the cliffs of Leucas, despondent over an unrequited love.

ANAKREON was born circa 570 BCE in the Ionian city of Teos. His poems survive mostly in quotations from subsequent poets in the *Greek Anthology,* many of whom imitated his style without capturing his incisive, self-deprecatory humor.

ASKLEPIADOS was born circa 320 BCE on the island of Samos. One of the earliest and best of the epigrammists, he revived meters unused since Sappho.

PRAXILLA'S few extant poems and fragments are found in the *Greek Anthology.*

RUFINUS'S dates are uncertain, like several of the poets in the *Greek Anthology.* His work survives in only a handful of lyric poems and fragments.

MARCUS ARGENTARIUS lived in the first century BCE.

GAIUS VALERIUS CATULLUS was born in Verona circa 84 BCE and died by the age of thirty. He is said to have modeled the "Lesbia" in his poems on the wife of a northern Italian governor. He both translated and stole from Sappho. One hundred and sixteen of his poems survive, famous for their passionate love and invective: *odi et amo,* "I hate and I love."

PHILODEMOS lived in Naples circa 75–35 BCE and was a popular and influential teacher of Epicurean philosophy.

OVID, whose full name was Publius Ovidius Naso, was born in an Apennine valley east of Rome in March 43 BCE. Augustus banished him in 8 CE and his books were removed from libraries, perhaps the result of Ovid's having published the great *Art of Love* and seducing the emperor's granddaughter. Before his death, he wrote about his ten years in exile.

PETRONIUS ARBITER (d. 66 CE) is the author of the *Satyricon,* a great satirist, and a member of Nero's inner circle.

TZU YEH may have been a "wineshop girl" in the fourth century CE, or she may have been a persona developed by several young women poets.

AGATHIAS SCHOLASTICUS was a Greek poet, historian, and lawyer (ca. 531–580) who lived in Constantinople. About a hundred of his poems are found in the *Greek Anthology.*

COMETAS CHARTULARIUS is known only by a handful of poems in the *Greek Anthology.* He is thought to have lived in the sixth century.

PAULUS SILENTIARIUS (d. ca. 575) was an epigrammist and an officer in the imperial household of the emperor Justinian.

LI PO (701–762), China's most famous poet, was imprisoned as a traitor, pardoned, exiled, celebrated, granted amnesty, and lived as a kind of knight-errant and miscreant. He wrote Taoist and Buddhist poems, panhandled, bragged, and drank himself to death. But his genius is undeniable. He was the most imaginative and original poet of the T'ang dynasty.

OTOMO NO YAKAMOCHI (718–785) was a major poet in the *Man'yoshu,* the first imperial poetry anthology of Japan, as well as one of its primary editors. He was Commanding General of the Eastern Armies and a great love poet.

YUAN CHEN (779–831) was a great and controversial poet banished for his humanistic philosophy and his refusal to remain silent about gross injustices.

His life is told in *The Dream of the Red Chamber*, a Yuan-dynasty drama.

LI HO (791–817) was labeled a mystical poet because of his many allusions to shamanistic practices. His poor health and radical political observations kept him from high office and probably saved him from exile.

ARIWARA NO NARIHIRA (825–880) was the fifth son of Prince Abo, who was the son of Emperor Heizei and Princess Ito. Handsome and self-indulgent, he is one of the "six poetic geniuses" of Japan and figures prominently in the classic *Tales of Ise*.

LI HSUN'S ancestry leads back to the Persians, but despite being less than "purely" Chinese, he achieved great influence at the court of the then-independent state of Shu in tenth-century Szechwan.

ONO NO KOMACHI (fl. ninth century) is the only female member of the "six poetic geniuses." Little is known of her biography, but several Noh dramas are based upon legends of her life.

IZUMI SHIKIBU (970–1030) was the daughter of a feudal lord and was sent to the Heian court to serve a former empress. Her famous diary chronicles life at court and her many loves, including at least two princes. Lady Murasaki records her animosity toward Izumi Shikibu in *Tale of Genji*.

LIU YUNG (987–1053) was an accomplished musician and a great lyrical poet who worked as a junior secretary in a local administration in Chekiang, living in abject, resolute poverty. His poems were sung throughout regional villages.

SAMUEL HA-NAGID (993–1056) was vizier to the King of Granada and, for eighteen years, commander of his armies. Ha-Nagid is known in Arabic as Ismai'il ibn Nagrela. Some say it was the influence of the more accepting attitude toward homosexuality in Arabic cultures that allowed ha-Nagid, who was Jewish, to write openly of his homosexual love.

OU-YANG HSIU (1007–1072) lost his father at four and grew up in extreme poverty. He became a quintessential Chinese statesman-scholar-poet and a patron of several very important younger poets, including Su Tung-p'o. He was the most revered love poet in all of China.

SU TUNG-P'O (1037–1101), also known as Su Shih, was deeply schooled in Taoism before becoming devoted to the study of Ch'an (Zen) Buddhism. He suffered political defeats and banishments to become one of the great poets of the Chinese Buddhist tradition.

LI CH'ING-CHAO (1084–1151) is often called the Empress of Song. She was one of the most brilliant and innovative poets of the Sung dynasty. After the early death of her husband, she eventually remarried, but her new husband proved abusive, so she risked everything and left him. Her courage, her sharp-tongued literary criticism, and her passionate poems portray a remarkably "liberated" woman for her time. Many Chinese think of her as the first feminist in Chinese history.

MAHADEVIYAKKA (twelfth century) left her arranged marriage to become an ecstatic devotee of Shiva.

JELALUDDIN RUMI (1207–1273) was a young professor of theology in Turkey when he encountered the wandering dervish Shamsuddin of Tabriz and was transformed into an ecstatic devotee. He was a prolific poet whose highly rhythmical verses became dances for whirling dervishes.

HSU TSAI-SSU (ca. 1300) was a Mongolian poet. Only a few poems survive.

FRANCESCO PETRARCH (1304–1374) is one of the most influential poets in all of history. He established the dominance of the ten- and eleven-syllable line in Renaissance European poetry. He is also one of the most mannered, cerebral, and difficult poets in the European tradition. He lived mostly under the patronage of wealthy Italians and died near Padua, where his house still stands.

IKKYU SOJUN (1394–1481) was a Zen master renowned for his teaching and for his frankly erotic poems and revolutionary *shakuhachi* music. Appointed headmaster at Japan's huge Buddhist training center, Daitokuji, in Kyoto, he resigned after nine days, denouncing the monks for hypocrisy and inviting them to argue their differences "in the whorehouses and sake parlors" where he could be found. At seventy, he scandalized the Buddhist community by moving his lover into his quarters in the temple. His sphere of influence included the tea ceremony, Noh drama, ink painting, calligraphy, and poetry, and he founded what became known as the "Red Thread" (or erotic) school of Zen.

KABIR, a great fifteenth-century mystic, was an ecstatic devotional poet who wrote thousands of verses. His songs are in the tradition of the *mahatma*—or "great souls"—who sing against tyranny and oppression, preaching tolerance between Hindu and Muslim communities.

VIDYAPATI was a fifteenth-century love poet who wrote in the eastern Indian language of Maithili. His poems present Radha and Krishna as perfectly idealized lovers offering their example for all humanity.

MIRABAI (1498–1550) was an Indian princess whose devotional poems are addressed to "the Dark One," Krishna, and are filled with erotic longing. Hers was a powerful voice against the continued oppression of women, the caste system, and lack of religious freedom. Her songs have made her a saint in Hindu, Sikh, and Muslim communities alike.

WILLIAM SHAKESPEARE (1564–1616) was a popular actor and playwright who was known among friends for what were called "his sugared sonnets," published without the author's consent. Scholars have been arguing over the correct order of his sonnet sequence since publication in 1609.

BIHARI (1595–1664) was court poet to a Rajasthani ruler. He wrote in the Braj dialect of Hindi. *Satasai* ("The Seven Hundred"), his best known work—a compilation of over seven hundred couplets—is often compared to the *Kama Sutra*. His poems explore all the aspects of love, from the purely erotic to the purely spiritual.

ROBERT HERRICK (1591–1674) was a goldsmith who received a master's degree from Cambridge and was ordained in 1623. He was well known as one of the "Sons of Ben" (Jonson) who spent his time in London taverns talking literature. When his single volume of twelve hundred poems was published in 1647, it was met with complete silence. His poems would remain unknown until the late nineteenth century.

ANNE BRADSTREET (1612–1672) is often called the first poet in the United States, and may have been the first professional woman poet in the English language. When her first book was published in London, she was hailed as "the Tenth Muse." She was a scholar of English, French, and classical literature and spoke out for the rights of Puritan women.

SE PRAJ (seventeenth century) was exiled from a Thai court because of his engagement with the many court women who swooned over his poems. While in exile he wrote a poem for another governor's mistress. Upon reading the poem, the governor had him beheaded.

ANDREW MARVELL (1621–1678) apparently worked as an obscure tutor until 1657, when he was appointed Assistant to the Latin Secretary for the Commonwealth, John Milton, whom Marvell may have saved from imprisonment or execution after the Restoration. In his lifetime, Marvell was known, if at all, as a minor satirist, his "serious" poetry being published only three years after his death.

JOHN DRYDEN (1631–1700) was a playwright, translator, and essayist whom Samuel Johnson called "the father of English criticism" for his development of the clear, simple, direct prose style that remains modern to this day. He is perhaps the greatest English satirical poet.

SOR JUANA INÉS DE LA CRUZ (1651–1695) was hailed in her time as "the Phoenix of Mexico, the Tenth Muse," but her poetry was forgotten upon her death, only to be rediscovered in this century. Octavio Paz has called her "the most neglected poet in the Americas."

JONATHAN SWIFT (1667–1745) was born in Dublin of English parents, but fled Ireland to live in London until he returned as a chaplain to the Lord Justice in 1699. For many years he was involved with educating and caring for a young woman, Esther Johnson, whom he loved all his life but never married. Increasing deafness caused by severe inner ear disorders isolated the satirist late in his life, and then senility set in; in 1742 guardians were appointed to look after his affairs until his death.

WILLIAM BLAKE (1757–1827) lived a life of almost total obscurity. He married an illiterate girl and taught her to read and to assist in his printing and engraving, but an unhappy marriage contributed to his attacks on possessive, jealous women in much of his early writing. His single bid for public recognition, a one-man show in 1809, was an utter failure. He nevertheless spent his life following his "Divine Vision," writing poems of ecstasy and agony protesting poverty and sexual and religious suppression, and printing his books (such as *Jerusalem*) in editions as small as five copies. The last ten years of his life, he gave up poetry to concentrate exclusively on his visual art. In Blake's universe, God exists within "the Universal Man." He declares "selfhood" the original sin. Whitman's "Song of Myself" is in many respects a response to Blake. Blake's stature as a major poet has been recognized only since the early twentieth century.

JOHN KEATS (1795–1821) lost his father at age eight and saw his mother die of tuberculosis when he was fourteen. At fifteen he was withdrawn from school and apprenticed with a surgeon, and at twenty he was qualified to practice as an apothecary. But he immediately left medicine to devote himself to poetry "for ten years, that I may overwhelm / Myself in poesy; so I may do the deed / That my own soul has to itself decreed." His poetry and letters reveal a mind that is almost Taoist in its fascination with inseparable but irreconcilable opposites, melancholy found in delight, ecstasy in grief, highest love approximating death. While advocating a life of "sensation," he also spoke for an aesthetics of detachment and for social responsibility. Like his mother and his younger brother whose last months he attended, Keats died of tuberculosis.

WALT WHITMAN (1819–1892) could find no publisher for his *Leaves of Grass,* so he published it himself (in 1855) and reviewed it himself under various pseudonyms. Stunned by his "barbaric yawp," the genteel poets and critics of his age were shocked by his directness, by his rude, red-dirt American speech. He spent the rest of his life adding to and revising his one great book of poems, essentially inventing the dominant style of American poetry to this day.

CHARLES BAUDELAIRE (1821–1867) was considered a failure in his lifetime. His poetry and art criticism were ignored or attacked as depraved. When *Les Fleurs du Mal* was published in 1857, it was reviled, and the poet, publisher, and printer convicted on charges of obscenity and fined. He is undoubtedly the greatest French poet of the nineteenth century.

EMILY DICKINSON (1830–1886) published virtually nothing in her lifetime, but left sixty little volumes of poems with her sister before she died. She did send a few poems to former pastor and essayist Thomas Wentworth Higginson, asking whether they "breathed." Otherwise, she lived quietly and imagined vigorously in a reclusive life in Massachusetts. It would take until 1955 for her complete poems to be published. She is, with Whitman, one of the two major American poets of the nineteenth century.

PAUL LAURENCE DUNBAR (1872–1906) was the son of slaves, whose father fled to Canada to escape slavery and whose mother was freed after the Civil War. He grew up in Dayton, Ohio, in a household where self-taught readers cherished volumes of history and poetry. His poetry draws from the blues-spiritual tradition as well as from his readings of European poetry. He became the first widely popular black poet in America.

ANTONIO MACHADO Y RUIZ (1875–1939) was born in Seville and raised in Madrid. Gaining a professorship in French, he moved to Soria, where his young wife died. For ten years he moved back and forth from Paris, finally settling in Madrid for part of each year. Perhaps because of the death of his wife, and certainly in part because of the rise of Generalissimo Franco's dictatorship and the banning of Machado's writing, the poet is famous for his poignant sense of solitude and a somber, unadorned style.

YOSANO AKIKO (1878–1942) could be called Japan's first feminist. A prolific writer of poetry, essays, novels, stories, fairytales, and autobiography, her first book, *Tangled Hair,* is a collection of *tanka* (five-line poems in traditional form) detailing the passions and heartaches of erotic love in a triangle. A great social conscience, she spoke out almost alone against Japanese expansionism. She remained in the forefront of the women's rights movement all her life.

ANNA AKHMATOVA (1889–1966) was born in Odessa on the Black Sea, but her name is forever linked to Petersburg and the village of Tsarskoye Selo, where she spent the first sixteen years of her life. The best of the Russian modernist poets, she would spend much of her life in enforced silence, a victim of censorship, her friends memorizing her poems in order to save them for posterity. A stoical, reticent woman, Akhmatova is revealed only through her poems and letters.

FEDERICO GARCÍA-LORCA (1898–1936) was born in Granada and was murdered by Franco's civil guard after refusing to leave Spain. He was a major poet and dramatist, a pianist, artist, actor, and director. He drew heavily on the folklore and traditions of Anadalusia, advocating a "poetry of deep song" imbued with soulful *duende,* writing "verses that are very much *my own,* singing the same way to Christ as to Buddha, to Mohammed as to Pan."

PABLO NERUDA (1904–1973) was a prolific *poeta del pueblo,* poet of the people, one of the dominant figures in twentieth-century Chilean history and recipient of the 1971 Nobel Prize for Literature. A dedicated political activist, he was an apologist for Stalinist Russia while remaining devoted to the ideals of democratic socialism. When he died, brokenhearted over the U.S.-inspired and -financed overthrow of the democratically elected socialist government of Allende in 1972, the new dictatorship issued an edict forbidding public acknowledgment of his funeral. Nevertheless, tens of thousands risked life and limb, pouring into the streets, chanting, "I am Pablo Neruda, I am Pablo Neruda!"

KENNETH REXROTH (1905–1982) was an autodidact, a conscientious objector during World War II, a primary figure in the San Francisco Renaissance, and author of fifty-four volumes of poetry, essays, translations from a dozen languages, plays, and autobiography. A poet with an enormous spiritual hunger, he drew equally from the classics, from Jewish intellectual traditions, and from Buddhist and Christian philosophical traditions.

SA'ID 'AQL (b. 1912) is a Lebanese poet who is best known for bringing the influence of French Symbolism into Arabic poetry.

THOMAS MCGRATH (1916–1990) was born on a North Dakota farm and served in the Aleutian Islands during World War II before accepting a Rhodes Scholarship at Oxford University. Blacklisted during the McCarthy Era for his socialist politics, McGrath worked as a documentary film-script writer, labor organizer, and teacher.

HAYDEN CARRUTH (b. 1921) received the National Book Critics Circle Award for his *Collected Shorter Poems 1946–1991*. The author of dozens of volumes of poetry and essays, he has addressed the meditative, the erotic, and the poet's responsibilities for nearly fifty years.

DENISE LEVERTOV (b. 1923) is a prolific poet whose meditative prowess is revealed alongside her profound social conscience and luminous powers of description in many volumes of poetry and essays. Born in England, she has lived in the United States since the 1950s, currently in Seattle.

CAROLYN KIZER (b. 1925) is a Pulitzer Prize–winning poet and the former director of the literature program at the National Endowment for the Arts. Her poetry and translations reveal the influence of time spent living in China and Pakistan. She has been a leading figure in feminist poetry for four decades.

ROBERT CREELEY (b. 1926), a leading figure at Black Mountain College in the 1950s, is one of the most popular and influential poets of our time.

ADRIENNE RICH (b. 1929) is the author of some of the most important poetry and essays of our time. In her poetry, which has been translated into dozens of languages, the erotic and the political, the spiritual and the physical, are mutually engaged in seamless lyrics.

ROBERTO SOSA (b. 1930) was born in Yoro, Honduras, and was raised in poverty under the dictatorship of Tiburcio Carias Andino. A teacher, journalist, and editor, he lives in Tegucigalpa, where his *Obra Completa* was published in 1990.

Robert Kelly (b. 1935) is a prolific poet, editor, and scholar formerly associated with the influential literary journals *Trobar* and *Chelsea Review.* He teaches at Bard College in Annandale-on-Hudson, New York.

LUCILLE CLIFTON (b. 1936) has twice been nominated for the Pulitzer Prize and has received an Emmy Award from the American Academy of Television Arts and Sciences. The author of several volumes of poetry that are among the most popular of our time, her most recent collection is *The Book of Light.*

JAAN KAPLINSKI (b. 1941) was born in Tartu, Estonia. His father disappeared into Stalin's labor camps while the poet was a small child. A student of structural and mathematical linguistics and of anthropology, he has translated from Spanish, French, English, and Polish, and is a leading figure in the cultural life of newly free Estonia.

SAM HAMILL (b. 1943) is the author of more than thirty volumes of poetry, essays, and translations from classical Chinese and Japanese, ancient Greek, Latin, and other languages. He is founding editor of Copper Canyon Press.

GIOCONDA BELLI (b. 1948) was born in Managua, Nicaragua, and gained international attention for her feminist, erotic, and political poems during the Sandinista movement. Exiled in 1975 for her ties to the national liberation movement, she lived in Costa Rica for three years. She now lives in Managua.

OLGA BROUMAS (b. 1949) was born in Syros, Greece, has published five volumes of poetry, and translated the poetry and essays of the Greek Nobel laureate Odysseas Elytis. Renowned for its lyric intensity, her poetry is rooted in the ecstatic tradition with Sappho as its wellspring.

MAURYA SIMON (b. 1950) was born in New York City and grew up in Europe and Southern California before studying Tamil in India. Her four volumes of published poetry reflect her extensive studies in Indo-European cultures, especially early Hindu and Buddhist traditions, along with her Jewish heritage.

DORIANNE LAUX (b. 1952) was born in Augusta, Maine, and is of Irish, French, and Algonquin Indian heritage. She lived in the San Francisco Bay area for more than ten years, holding down a succession of menial jobs while perfecting her craft, earning a degree from Mills College, and raising her daughter. She teaches at the University of Oregon in Eugene.

CREDITS

A<small>LL TRANSLATIONS</small> are my own except as noted.
Translations from ancient Greek, Chinese,
Japanese, Latin, Spanish and Estonian are from orig-
inal sources. Translations used in making original
versions include the following: Franz Boas, "Eskimo
Tales and Songs," *Journal of American Folk-lore,*
1894–97; Franz Boas, "Songs of the Kwakiutl Indi-
ans," *Bureau of Ethnography,* 1896; *Somali Poetry,* by
B. W. Andrzejewski and I. M. Lewis (New York: Ox-
ford University Press, 1964); *Songs of Kabir* by Nirmal
Dass (Albany: State University of New York Press,
1991); *Interpretive Translations of Thai Poets,* by M. R.
Seni Pramoj (Thai Watana Panich Company, 1986).

Grateful acknowledgment is due to New Direc-
tions Publishing Corp. for permission to reprint
poems from *The Infinite Moment: Poems from Ancient
Greek,* copyright © 1992; to Shambhala Publications
for permission to reprint poems from *Only Compan-
ion: Japanese Poems of Love and Longing,* copyright
© 1992, and from *Midnight Flute: Chinese Poems of
Love and Longing,* copyright © 1994; to Blue Begonia
Press for permission to reprint poems from *Catullus
Redivivus,* copyright © 1986. Anonymous Egyptian:
"He is the love-wolf . . ." from *Love Lyrics of Ancient*

Egypt, translated by Barbara Hughes Fowler. Copyright © 1994 by the University of North Carolina Press. Used by permission of the publisher. Samuel ha-Nagid: *Exiled In The Word,* translated by Jerome Rothenberg and Harris Lenowitz, copyright © 1989, published by Copper Canyon Press and reprinted by permission. Ou-yang Hsiu: *Love and Time,* translated by J. P. Seaton, copyright © 1989, published by Copper Canyon Press and reprinted by permission. Mahadeviyakka: *Women in Praise of the Sacred,* edited by Jane Hirshfield, copyright © 1994, published by Harper Collins and reprinted by permission. Jelaluddin Rumi: *Like This,* versions by Coleman Barks, copyright © 1990, published by Maypop and reprinted by permission. Vidyapati: *Love Songs of Vidyapati,* translated by Deben Bhattacharya and edited by W. G. Archer, copyright © 1963, published by George Allen & Unwin Ltd. and reprinted by permission. Mirabai: *For Love of the Dark One,* translated by Andrew Schelling, copyright © 1993, published by Shambhala Publications and reprinted by permission. Sor Juana Inés de la Cruz: *A Sor Juana Anthology,* translated by Alan S. Trueblood, copyright © 1988, published by Harvard University Press and reprinted by permission. Charles Baudelaire: *Les Fleurs du Mal,* translated by Richard Howard, copyright © 1982 by Richard Howard, published by David R. Godine and reprinted by permission. Antonio Machado: *Antonio Machado: Selected Poems and Prose,* translated by Robert Bly, edited by Dennis Maloney, copyright © 1983. Reprinted with permission from White Pine Press, Fredonia, New York. Anna Akhmatova: *Poems of Akhmatova,* selected, translated, and introduced by Stanley Kunitz with Max Hayward, copyright © 1973, published by Atlantic-Little, Brown and reprinted by permission. Pablo Neruda: "Body of a Woman," from *Twenty Love Poems and the Song of Despair,* translated by W. S. Merwin, copyright © 1969, published by Jonathan Cape Ltd., reprinted by permission of the poet; "Love Song," from *The Yellow Heart,* translated by William O'Daly, copyright © 1990, published by Copper Canyon Press and reprinted by permission. Kenneth Rexroth: *Collected Shorter Poems,* copyright © 1940 by Kenneth Rexroth. Reprinted by permission of New Directions Publishing Corp. Sa'id 'Aql: *Modern Arabic Poetry, An Anthology,* edited by Salma Khadra Jayyusi, copyright © 1987 by Columbia University Press. Reprinted with permission of the publisher. Thomas McGrath: *Selected Poems: 1938–1988,* copyright © 1988, published by Copper Canyon Press and reprinted by permission. Hayden Carruth: *Collected Shorter Poems: 1946–1991,* copyright © 1992, published by Copper Canyon Press and reprinted by permission. Denise Levertov: *Poems 1960–1967,* copyright © 1966 by Denise Levertov. Reprinted by permission of New Directions Publishing Corp. Carolyn Kizer: *The Nearness of You,* copyright © 1986, published by Copper Canyon Press and reprinted by permission. Robert Creeley: *The Collected Poems of Robert Creeley, 1945–1975,* copyright © 1982, published by University of California Press and reprinted by permission. Adrienne Rich: *The Fact of a Doorframe: Poems Selected and New, 1950–1984,* by permission of the author and W. W. Norton & Company, Inc. Copyright © 1984 by Adrienne Rich. Copyright © 1975, 1978 by W. W. Norton & Company, Inc. © 1981 by Adrienne Rich. Roberto Sosa: *The Common Grief,* translated by Jo Anne Engelbert, copyright © 1994, published by Curbstone Press and reprinted by permission. Robert Kelly: *Finding the Measure,* copyright © 1968, published by Black Sparrow Press and reprinted by permission. Lucille Clifton: *The Book of Light,* copyright © 1993, published by Copper Canyon Press and reprinted by permission. Jaan Kaplinski: *The Wandering Border,* copyright © 1987, published by Copper Canyon Press and reprinted by permission. Gioconda Belli: *From Eve's Rib,* translated by Steven F. White, copyright © 1989, published by Curbstone Press and reprinted by permission. Olga Broumas: *Perpetua,* copyright © 1989, published by Copper Canyon Press and reprinted by permission. Maurya Simon: "Shiva's Prowess," copyright © 1994, printed by permission of the author. Dorianne Laux: *What We Carry,* copyright © 1995, published by BOA and reprinted by permission.

SHAMBHALA LIBRARY